Chic & Unique
WEDDING
Cakes

30 MODERN DESIGNS FOR ROMANTIC CELEBRATIONS

Chic & Unique WEDDING *Cakes*

ZOE CLARK

D&C

David and Charles

www.bakeme.com

A DAVID & CHARLES BOOK
© F&W Media International, LTD 2012

David & Charles is an imprint of F&W Media International, LTD
Brunel House, Forde Close, Newton Abbot, TQ12 4PU, UK

F&W Media International, LTD is a subsidiary of F+W Media Inc.
4700 East Galbraith Road, Cincinnati, OH 45236, USA

First published in the UK and USA in 2012

Text and designs © Zoe Clark 2012
Layout and photography © F&W Media International, LTD 2012

A catalogue record for this book is available from the
British Library.

ISBN-13: 978-1-4463-0204-0 hardback
ISBN-10: 1-4463-0204-0 hardback

ISBN-13: 978-1-4463-0163-0 paperback
ISBN-10: 1-4463-0163-X paperback

Printed in China by RR Donnelley
for F&W Media International, LTD
Brunel House, Forde Close, Newton Abbot, TQ12 4PU, UK

10 9 8 7 6 5 4 3 2 1

Publisher Alison Myer
Acquisitions Editor Jennifer Fox-Proverbs
Desk Editor Jeni Hennah
Project Editor Heather Haynes
Design Manager Sarah Clark
Art Editor Sarah Underhill
Photographer Sian Irvine
Senior Production Controller Kelly Smith

F+W Media Inc. publishes high-quality books on a wide
range of subjects. For more great book ideas visit:
www.bakeme.com

Contents

INTRODUCTION

This book on wedding cakes has been one I've wanted to write for a long time. Being a self-confessed romantic has meant that being able to design and create these ten fabulous wedding cakes has been a dream for me.

Designing wedding cakes and confections gives me immense pleasure and is really what I do best. Being part of a couple's special day is a real privilege and designing a cake that reflects their wedding theme is very important. To me, there is nothing more beautiful than a tiered cake covered with lace piping and adorned with beautiful sugar flowers, but there are a host of other ways to decorate a wedding cake, many of which I have included in this book.

This book is divided into ten chapters, each featuring one main wedding cake accompanied by two complementary designs, including cookies, cupcakes and fondant fancies, which can be added to the wedding feast, or made as favours for the guests. The projects have all been inspired by an element of the wedding itself – the flowers, the dress, the shoes, and even the venue – to continue and develop the theme of the big day.

The cakes are shaped around three or four, and occasionally five, tiers, but can easily be scaled down if desired. Step-by-step instructions are included for reproducing the ten main designs, which include such techniques as elegant brush embroidery, stencilling with icing and making hand-crafted sugar flowers. A separate section on recipes and techniques outlines quantities required and basic recipes for making fruit, carrot, chocolate and sponge cakes, as well as wedding cake essentials such as covering cakes with icing, assembling cake tiers and using a piping bag.

Each chapter is introduced by showing exactly where my inspiration has come from and hopefully this will inspire you to create your own designs to match the requirements of your own occasion. The beautiful styling and photography not only show how these elements tie in with the design but can also give you ideas on how to display your cake on the day.

I hope this book not only teaches you the various skills to achieve the different designs but most of all gives you inspiration to go on to create your own unique wedding cake. So, whether you're a first time baker or a qualified professional, I hope you have as much fun and pleasure making your wedding cake as I did designing and creating these.

Good luck!

TOOLS AND EQUIPMENT

The following basic tools are essential for baking the cakes in this book.
It is important to have all your tools and equipment to hand before you start baking.

Baking essentials

❖ **Large electric mixer** for making cakes, buttercream (frosting) and royal icing

❖ **Kitchen scales** for weighing out ingredients

❖ **Measuring spoons** for measuring small quantities

❖ **Mixing bowls** for mixing ingredients

❖ **Spatulas** for mixing and gently folding together cake mixes

❖ **Cake tins** for baking cakes

❖ **Tartlet tins and/or muffin trays** for baking cupcakes

❖ **Baking trays** for baking cookies

❖ **Wire racks** for cooling cakes and icing fondant fancies

GENERAL EQUIPMENT

❖ **Greaseproof (wax) paper or baking parchment** for lining tins and to use under icing during preparation

❖ **Clingfilm (plastic wrap)** for covering icing to prevent drying out and for wrapping cookie dough

❖ **Large non-stick board** to put icing on when rolling it out

❖ **Non-slip mat** to put under the board so that it doesn't slip on the work surface

❖ **Large and small non-stick rolling pins** for rolling out icing and marzipan

❖ **Large and small sharp knife** for cutting and shaping icing

❖ **Large serrated knife** for carving and sculpting cakes

❖ **Cake leveller** for cutting even, level layers of sponge

❖ **Cake card** is a special card, thinner than a cake board, to which you can attach miniature cakes

❖ **Large and small palette knife** for applying buttercream (frosting) and ganache

❖ **Icing or marzipan spacers** to give a guide to the thickness of icing and marzipan when rolling out

❖ **Icing smoothers** for smoothing icing

❖ **Spirit level** for checking that cakes are level when stacking them

❖ **Metal ruler** for measuring different heights and lengths

❖ **Cake scraper** to scrape and smooth buttercream (frosting), ganache or royal icing, used in a similar way to a palette knife

Creative tools

- ❧ **Hollow plastic dowels** for assembling cakes

- ❧ **Turntable** for layering cakes

- ❧ **Double-sided tape** to attach ribbon around cakes, boards and pillars

- ❧ **Piping (pastry) bags** for royal icing decorations

- ❧ **Piping tubes (tips)** for piping royal icing

- ❧ **Cocktail sticks (toothpicks) or cel sticks** for colouring and curling icing

- ❧ **Acetate or cellophane sheets** for run-out icing decorations, or for covering icing if you are interrupted while working to keep it from drying out

- ❧ **Edible glue** for sticking icing to icing

- ❧ **Edible pens** for marking positioning guides

- ❧ **Needle scriber** for lightly scoring positioning guides and bursting bubbles in icing

- ❧ **Cake-top marking template** for finding/marking the centre of cakes and marking where dowels should be placed

- ❧ **Pastry brush** for brushing sugar syrup and apricot masking spread or strained jam (jelly) on to cakes

- ❧ **Fine paintbrushes** for gluing and painting

- ❧ **Dusting brushes** for brushing edible dust on to icing

- ❧ **Dipping fork** for dipping fondant fancies in fondant icing

- ❧ **Ball tool** for frilling or thinning the edge of flower (petal/gum) paste

- ❧ **Foam pad** for softening and frilling flower (petal/gum) paste

- ❧ **Frill cutters** for cutting borders and pretty edges

- ❧ **Blossom, petal and star plunger cutters** for cutting blossoms, petals and stars

- ❧ **Circle cutters** for cutting circles of various sizes

- ❧ **Shaped cutters** for cutting out shapes such as leaves, diamonds, stars and wedding cakes

DUSKY ROSE ROMANCE

The inspiration for this beautiful theme came from a bridal magazine; a gorgeous feature caught my eye as it combined all my favourite 'girlie' colours. The soft pink pastel and dusky purple hues of the flowers and the bridal gown toned perfectly with the hints of silver in the tableware.

A delightful flower girl dress by designer Nicki MacFarlane is the inspiration behind the sweet dotty theme running through the projects in this chapter. The handcrafted roses and purple-coloured eucalyptus bring an element of sophistication and class to the style.

"*Sweet but sophisticated, cute but classy, this pink pastel cake is a bride's dream*"

Sweet roses and dots

Roses are by far the most common sugar flower found on wedding cakes. I prefer to make large unwired roses which are attached to the cake when the outer petals are still semi-soft so they can be shaped to sit nicely together. In contrast, the purple-dusted eucalyptus sprigs have been individually wired and are just poked in and amongst the roses. Rose cones need to be made 24 hours in advance of decorating the cake.

MATERIALS

❖ One 10cm (4in) round cake, one 18cm (7in) round cake and one 25cm (10in) round cake, each 10cm (4in) deep, prepared and iced in pale dusky pink sugarpaste (rolled fondant) (see Covering Cakes)

❖ One 35cm (14in) round cake board, covered with pale dusky pink sugarpaste (rolled fondant) (see Icing Cake Boards)

❖ 600g (1lb 5oz) white flower (petal/gum) paste

❖ Edible glue

❖ Paste food colourings: wine purple, dusky pink, green

❖ Edible dust: dusky pink, wine purple, green, aubergine

❖ Half quantity of royal icing

EQUIPMENT

❖ 7 hollow pieces of dowel cut to size (see Assembling Tiered Cakes)

❖ 10mm ($^3/_8$in) white satin ribbon

❖ 4mm ($^1/_8$in) small circle cutter

❖ Cocktail sticks (toothpicks)

❖ Large polystyrene cake dummy

❖ 5cm (2in) and 6cm (2$^1/_2$in) rose petal cutters

❖ Foam pad

❖ Ball tool

❖ Paint palette

❖ Dusting brushes

❖ 26 and 20 gauge wire

❖ Grooved board (optional)

❖ 1.5cm ($^5/_8$in) and 2cm ($^3/_4$in) small oval cutters

❖ Small rose petal veiner

❖ Green florist tape

❖ 15mm ($^5/_8$in) white, double-faced satin ribbon

❖ Double-sided tape

1 Dowel and assemble the three tiers on to the cake board (see Assembling Tiered Cakes).

2 Wrap a length of 10mm (³/8in) ribbon around the base of each tier and secure with double-sided tape.

3 Thinly roll out a small amount of white flower (petal/gum) paste and cut out dots with the small circle cutter. You will need enough dots to make four rows horizontally and vertically around each tier. Using edible glue, stick the dots on to the cake tiers, leaving approximately 3cm (1¹/4in) between each one.

TIP

Use only a minimal amount of glue so you can move the dots if necessary to ensure they all line up correctly.

4 To make the roses, roll approximately 15g (¹/2oz) of white flower (petal/gum) paste into a ball and shape it into a cone. Insert a cocktail stick (toothpick) into the base and stick it into a polystyrene cake dummy to dry for at least 24 hours. Repeat to make two more cones.

5 Colour 200g (7oz) of flower (petal/gum) paste with purple paste food colouring to make the three lilac roses. Thinly roll out the paste and cut out 12 petals using the small rose petal cutter. Place the petals on to the foam pad and use the ball tool to soften the edges. Wrap one petal around each of the three cones and stick them in place with a small amount of edible glue. Next place three petals around the centre petal on each of the three cones.

6 Roll out some more flower (petal/gum) paste and cut out three more petals per rose to make the next layer. Soften the edges of the paste and, using a cocktail stick (toothpick), curl back the petals before attaching them to the cone. Try to tuck one side of each petal into the next so they look like they are all wrapped around each other.

7 Make five more petals per rose as before for the fourth layer and secure them in place with edible glue. The fifth and final layer is made using seven petals cut from the large rose petal cutter. These petals need to be slightly drier and stiffer so they are easier to handle and don't flop down when you attach them to the flower. Sit them in a paint palette to semi-shape them until they are ready to handle.

8 Colour 200g (7oz) of flower (petal/gum) paste dusky pink and make three roses as described above. Colour 140g (5oz) of flower (petal/gum) paste a deeper purple/pink to make the two remaining roses. Dust each rose with matching coloured edible dust to make them look more realistic. Attach the flowers to the cake, securing them in place with some dusky pink royal icing; there are four flowers on the top and two on the ledges. Make a few more petals in each of the three colours to fill any large gaps between the flowers.

9 Colour the remaining flower (petal/gum) paste pale green and cut the 26 gauge wire into 10cm (4in) pieces. Roll out a small piece of the paste, leaving a thick ridge down the centre for the wire. You can use a grooved board to do this or simply start with a sausage shape and roll outwards from the centre. Cut out the leaf using a small oval cutter, then insert the wire and press it into the rose petal veiner. Pinch the leaf slightly at the bottom and set aside to dry. Repeat to make three further small leaves and 4 large leaves per stem.

10 Dust the leaves with green and aubergine edible dust. Tape two small leaves together to a 15cm (6in) piece of 20 gauge wire using florist tape. Tape two more small leaves together further down the stem followed by four more large leaves, again in pairs. Repeat this to make six stems in total. Dust the tape around the stem with edible aubergine dust.

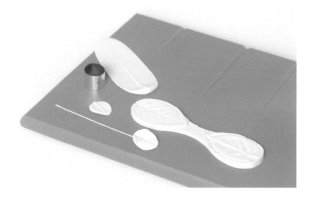

11 Trim the eucalyptus stems and poke them in between each rose. Secure them in place with a small amount of pale dusky pink royal icing. Finish by securing a length of 15mm (5/8in) white satin ribbon around the base board using double-sided tape.

Eucalyptus cupcakes

Complement the main cake by creating these gorgeous cupcakes, some decorated with dots and some with eucalyptus leaves. Rather than using wires, pipe on the eucalyptus stems so the cupcakes are completely edible and you don't have to pick anything off.

To make the spotty cupcakes, cut tiny dots from thinly rolled-out white flower (petal/gum) paste using the no. 4 piping tube (tip). Stick them on to the cupcakes using a small amount of edible glue.

To make the eucalyptus cupcakes, colour some royal icing with the dusky pink and purple food colouring and, using a no. 2 piping tube (tip) in a small piping (pastry) bag, pipe stems on to the cupcakes. Attach the eucalyptus leaves in pairs along the stems using coloured royal icing.

YOU'LL ALSO NEED

❖ Cupcakes in silver cases covered with sugarpaste (rolled fondant) to match the colour of the main cake (see Covering Cupcakes with Sugarpaste)

❖ Unwired eucalyptus leaves made as for the main project

❖ Nos. 2 and 4 piping tubes (tips)

Wedding cake cookies

These stylish matching wedding cake cookies, decorated to echo the design of the actual cake, are simple to make. Display them in a pretty china dish at each guest's table setting as an unusual gift.

Using the blossom cutter, cut out four flowers per cookie from pale purple flower (petal/gum) paste. Cut a few of the flowers in half for the flower at the top of the cake that sits behind the flower at the front. Stick the flowers on to the cookie with a small amount of edible glue. Cut the small dots from white flower (petal/gum) paste using the no. 4 piping tube (tip) and stick them on to the cookie. Finish by piping the detail on the flowers in a deeper purple and the lines at the base of each tier in white using a no. 1 piping tube (tip).

YOU'LL ALSO NEED

✤ Wedding cake cookies cut using the template (see Templates) and flooded with pale dusky pink royal icing (see Royal-Iced Cookies)

✤ Small blossom cutter

✤ Nos. 1 and 2 piping tubes (tips)

DAMASK ELEGANCE

Damask print has really come back into fashion in the last few years and makes a lovely theme for a modern wedding, especially if pale pastel colours are used. The talented girls at Dottie Creations design a wide range of contemporary stationery and the cakes and cookies here are inspired by one of my favourite collections, Darcy.

Using a stencilling technique is a great way to recreate intricate, repetitive patterns like damask as a piece of edible art. Stencilling on to icing is simple to do once you get the hang of it and is surprisingly effective.

"Pale green damask adds a touch of crisp, contemporary elegance to a wedding cake"

Stencil damask cake

The pale green and ivory colours of the cake match the invitation used as the inspiration for this chapter. However, you can adapt the colour of the icing, or use another damask or stencil design to suit the colour scheme and theme of your special occasion. The technique used is still the same.

MATERIALS

* One 10cm (4in) square cake, one 18cm (7in) square cake and one 25cm (10in) square cake, each 10cm (4in) deep, prepared and iced in green sugarpaste (rolled fondant) at least 24 hours in advance (see Covering Cakes)

* One quantity of royal icing

* Paste food colourings: ivory, green (I used a combination of mint, gooseberry and willow green)

* One 33cm (13in) square cake board, covered with green sugarpaste (rolled fondant) (see Icing Cake Boards)

EQUIPMENT

* Needle scriber

* Ruler or measuring tape

* Damp cloth or kitchen (paper) towel

* Damask stencil (Designer Stencils)

* Palette knife or cake scraper

* 8 hollow pieces of dowel cut to size (see Assembling Tiered Cakes)

* Icing smoothers

* Small piping (pastry) bag and no. 2 piping tube (tip)

* 15mm (5/8in) ivory satin ribbon

* Double-sided tape

* Fresh non-toxic flower to decorate (optional)

* Cake stand

TIP

When layering and preparing the cake, try to make sure your cakes are as angular as possible and the edges are really sharp.

1 Start by accurately and carefully marking the centre of each side on all three tiers, using a needle scriber and ruler.

2 Colour approximately two-thirds of the royal icing pale ivory and keep it covered with a damp cloth or piece of kitchen (paper) towel to prevent it from drying out while you decorate the cake.

3 Raise the cake up slightly on a board so the damask pattern can come nearly all the way down to the bottom of the cake. Place the stencil against the side of one of the cakes and, using a palette knife or cake scraper, thinly smear the ivory icing across the whole pattern. Try not to move the stencil while doing this or the icing will smudge.

4 Carefully and cleanly remove the stencil from the side of the cake to reveal the damask pattern. Use a damp fine paintbrush to fix or remove any stray icing left behind.

Ask someone to help you hold the cake in place with an icing smoother while you stencil on it, to prevent it from slipping.

5 Repeat this process around all the sides of the cake. Blend the corners of the cake as neatly as possible using a damp paintbrush.

6 Repeat this process to stencil the other two tiers and set them aside to dry.

7 Dowel and assemble the three tiers on to the 33cm (13in) cake board (see Assembling Tiered Cakes). Try to be as accurate as possible when assembling the cake as you don't want to have to move the tiers too much once they are in position as it might damage the pattern. If you find you need to move the tiers, use two smoothers and apply even pressure down the opposite sides of the cake to do this.

8 Colour some more royal icing with green paste food colouring to match the base icing colour of the cake. Do this gradually and keep checking the colour next to the cake. Place a no. 2 piping tube (tip) into a small piping (pastry) bag and fill it with the icing. Pipe a snail trail border around the base of each tier (see Piping with Royal Icing).

9 Wrap a length of ivory satin ribbon around the base board, securing with double-sided tape, and place a fresh flower on the top of the cake (optional). Finish by placing the cake on a cake stand and tie a bow around its stem to match the invitation.

Gift box mini cakes

These adorable little gift box mini cakes with a sugar bow make lovely favours to give to your guests. This sweet design is really versatile and can also be made for birthdays, christenings and even Christmas, simply by changing the colour scheme.

Roll out the flower (petal/gum) paste very thinly. Cut four strips approximately 10–12cm (4–4½in) long and 1cm (³⁄₈in) wide. Stick two of the strips on either side of the cake and trim at the top where they meet in the middle. Repeat this for the other two sides of the cake but this time pinch the ends where they meet together at the top before trimming them. Cut two strips approximately 5cm (2in) long for the bow's tails. Pinch them at one end and cut them on an angle at the other. Attach the pinched end to the centre of the cake to go under the bow. Cut a 16cm (6¼in) strip for the bow. Pinch the centre and the ends and curl them inwards to make the two loops. Stick them in place with edible glue. Make the knot using another strip, 4cm (1½in) long and folded over along the edges. Wrap it around the loops in the centre and attach to the cake.

YOU'LL ALSO NEED

- ✤ 5cm (2in) square cakes iced in ivory sugarpaste (rolled fondant) (see Miniature Cakes)
- ✤ Green flower (petal/gum) paste
- ✤ Edible glue

Damask cookies

The damask pattern can also be recreated on cookies, which make beautifully intricate and delicate squares to complement the rest of the range. Wrap damask stencil cookies in cellophane and tie with a satin bow for your guests to take away.

Colour the royal icing with green paste food colouring. Place the stencil on top of the cookie and, using a palette knife, thinly smear over the royal icing until the pattern is covered. Carefully remove the stencil and set aside to dry. Pipe a snail trail border around the sides of the cookies (see Piping with Royal Icing) using a no. 1.5 piping tube (tip).

YOU'LL ALSO NEED

❖ 7.5cm (3in) square cookies flooded with ivory royal icing (see Royal-Iced Cookies)

❖ Small damask stencil (Designer Stencils)

❖ No. 1.5 piping tube (tip)

❖ Cellophane bags and satin ribbon (optional)

CITY WEDDING

A city-themed wedding is a great way to celebrate a place that couples getting married hold close to their hearts. The talented team at Cutture make exquisite, bespoke, laser-cut skyline wedding stationery for couples to achieve exactly this. To reproduce this idea on a wedding cake, run-out decorations were made using templates of city landmarks and famous buildings.

For the projects in this chapter I have chosen London, where I now live and work, and Paris, probably the most romantic city in the world and which I am also very fond of. However, you can easily personalise the cake to represent your special place by choosing and making your own templates.

"A truly fabulous idea for a wedding cake, ideal for the modern metropolitan couple"

Skyline cake

A hexagonal-shaped cake makes a perfect canvas to support the fine run-out decorations, as the sides are flat and visible from the front. Outline and flood the buildings to get the main shape then, when they are dry, over-pipe basic details to make them more interesting. You will need to make your own templates in advance, taking care to make them the right size for the cake.

MATERIALS

❖ One 10cm (4in) hexagonal cake, one 15cm (6in) hexagonal cake, one 20cm (8in) hexagonal cake and one 23cm (9in) hexagonal cake, all 10cm (4in) deep, iced in pale grey sugarpaste (rolled fondant) (see Covering Cakes)

❖ One 35cm (14in) round or hexagonal cake board, covered in pale grey sugarpaste (rolled fondant) (see Icing Cake Boards)

❖ White fat

❖ 1–2 quantities of royal icing

❖ Paste food colouring: black

EQUIPMENT

❖ Paper for templates

❖ 6–8 large sheets of acetate

❖ Small and medium-sized piping (pastry) bags and nos.1, 1.5 and 2 piping tubes (tips)

❖ 10 hollow pieces of dowel cut to size (see Assembling Tiered Cakes)

❖ 15mm (5/8in) bridal white, satin ribbon

❖ Double-sided tape

1 Start by making your own templates. Find images of buildings or landmarks of the city of your choice. Trace over these and change their size as desired so you can play around with the placement of the buildings when you stick them on the cake. Make at least 10 to 15 outlines on paper of various feature buildings, which can be repeated around the cake, and another 10 to 15 different-sized building-like blocks, which can be used to fill any empty spaces.

2 Lightly grease the sheets of acetate, place them on a flat surface and slide one of the templates underneath. Colour approximately 8 tablespoons of royal icing with a touch of black paste food colouring so it is slightly paler than the colour of the cake.

3 Prepare the piping (pastry) bags. Fill a small piping (pastry) bag fitted with a no.1.5 tube (tip) with approximately 2 tablespoons of soft peak icing (see Soft Peak Royal Icing) and set aside for a moment while you thin down the remaining coloured icing to a flooding consistency (see 'Run-Out' Icing). Put the runny icing into medium piping (pastry) bags and set aside. If you are flooding in very small areas, use a no.1 piping tube (tip) inserted into a bag to squeeze out any tiny air bubbles and avoid any icing sinking.

4 Using the piping (pastry) bag of soft peak icing, pipe an outline over the template. Carefully move the template to one side and pipe over another outline. Repeat this at least two or three more times so you have enough for the cake, allowing for breakages.

TIP

Print images from the internet, resize them if necessary and trace them to help make your own templates.

5 Snip a small hole in the bag of the runny icing and fill in the outlines of the buildings. Repeat this for at least half of all the different-shaped buildings. Be careful not to bend the acetate sheet as you slide the templates around underneath it, as it will cause cracking of any run-outs that are starting to dry.

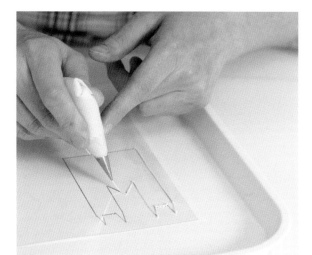

6 Repeat step 5 with white royal icing, using the remaining templates. The run-out decorations need to be made at least 24 hours in advance to allow enough time for them to dry before sticking them on the cake.

7 When the run-outs are completely dry, use a no. 1 piping tube (tip) to pipe lines for the details using soft peak royal icing in the same colour as the flooded decoration. You might find it easier to cut the acetate between the run-outs before doing this but take care not to break them, especially the more delicate shapes. Set aside to dry.

8 Dowel and assemble the four hexagonal cakes on top of the iced cake board (see Assembling Tiered Cakes). Use four dowels in the base tier and three in both the 20cm (8in) and 15cm (6in) tiers.

9 Carefully peel off the run-outs from the acetate. Do this by bringing the edge of the acetate towards you at the edge of a board or bench and peeling it downwards. Don't force the run-out off the sheet. Run a very small knife underneath it if it is still a bit wet to help release it.

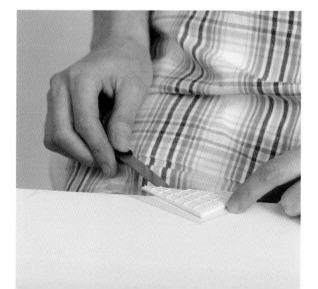

10 Start sticking the first layer of run-outs on to the cake. Using stiff royal icing, attach the pale grey decorations on the cake. Think about how you place them as you go. You don't want any of the shapes to stick out at the corners. Don't worry if there are any small gaps between buildings as you can cover this with the next layer.

11 Next stick the top layer (white run-outs) on and around the cake, covering over any gaps and filling in any areas that look too bare. If there are any buildings or landmarks with fine wires or suspended features (for example, the sides of Tower Bridge) pipe these details on to the cake after you have stuck everything on.

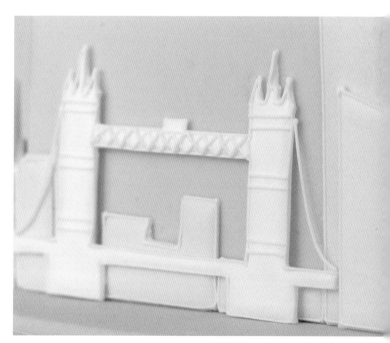

12 Finish by securing a length of 15mm (5⁄8in) bridal white, satin ribbon around the base board and secure in place with double-sided tape.

Landmark fancies

Decorate fondant fancies with different buildings and landmarks to serve alongside the main cake. Use a deeper grey colour for the icing and serve the fancies in silver cases to add more contrast against the white run-outs so they really stand out.

Stick the run-outs on to the fancies with a small amount of royal icing. Put some of the decorations on at an angle if you think they will look better.

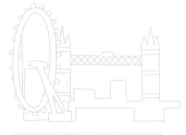

YOU'LL ALSO NEED

❖ 4cm (1½in) square fondant fancies dipped in medium grey fondant (see Fondant Fancies) and set in silver cases

❖ Small, white run-out decorations (see main project)

Landmark cookies

Hexagonal-shaped cookies with piped stripes and criss-cross patterns fit in perfectly with the city theme. Wrap them in cellophane bags and tie with ribbon to give away to your guests.

Fill a small piping (pastry) bag fitted with a no.1 piping tube (tip) with soft peak icing. Pipe an outline around the cookie, then carefully pipe straight lines across. Leave some with lines going one way and make a criss-cross pattern for others. When the lines are dry, stick on the run-outs with royal icing. Leave until completely dry before wrapping them in cellophane bags and tying with striped ribbon.

YOU'LL ALSO NEED
- Cookies cut using hexagonal template (see Templates), outlined and flooded with white royal icing
- Small, pale grey run-out decorations of buildings (see main project)
- Cellophane bags and striped ribbon (optional)

JEWELLED SPLENDOUR

After the wedding dress, the bride's shoes and accessories are the next most important choices for the big day. Most brides want to feel like a princess or at least feel special on their wedding day so their choice of outfit and how they accessorise it is vital.

My favourite shoe designer, Emmy, makes customised contemporary and feminine footwear and accessories which often feature beads or flowers in their design. The projects in this chapter have been inspired by these designs and created to match this theme, allowing a bride to match the cake with her shoes.

"*Subtle pink icing offset with elegant rows of pearls and beads makes for a truly feminine cake*"

Cake jewellery

The wedding cake is inspired by Emmy's 'Honey' shoe which incorporates her signature pink pattern on the inside of the shoe. The middle and ankle straps of the shoe incorporate pearls and beads in linked oval shapes, and this is the element of the design I have used to decorate the middle tier of the cake.

MATERIALS

- One 15cm (6in) round cake, 10cm (4in) deep, prepared and iced in pale dusky pink sugarpaste (rolled fondant) at least 12–24 hours in advance (see Covering Cakes)
- One 20cm (8in) round cake, 18cm (7in) deep, prepared and iced in pale dusky pink sugarpaste (rolled fondant) at least 12–24 hours in advance (see Covering Cakes)
- One 28cm (11in) round cake, 12cm (4½in) deep, prepared and iced in pale dusky pink sugarpaste (rolled fondant) at least 12–24 hours in advance (see Covering Cakes)
- One 35cm (14in) round cake board, covered with pale dusky pink sugarpaste (rolled fondant) at least 12–24 hours in advance (see Icing Cake Boards)
- Quarter quantity of royal icing
- 100g (3½oz) dusky pink flower (petal/gum) paste
- Edible glue
- 100g (3½oz) grey flower (petal/gum) paste
- 100g (3½oz) ivory flower (petal/gum) paste
- Edible dust colours: silver, pearl white
- Large and small pearl and silver dragees
- Opal coarse sugar sprinkles

EQUIPMENT

- 6 hollow pieces of dowel cut to size (see Assembling Tiered Cakes)
- Endless garret frill cutter
- Acetate sheets
- No. 3 piping tube (tip)
- Oval templates (see Templates)
- 43mm (1½in) and 65mm (2½in) circle cutters
- Dusting brush
- Tweezers
- Stitching tool
- White florist tape
- Half-bunch of large, pearl-head stamen
- Grooved non-stick board
- Large and small peony petal cutters and veiners
- 26-gauge white wire, cut into 10cm (4in) pieces
- Veining tool
- Shallow cupped mould or apple tray
- Heavy-duty pliers
- Flower pick
- Foam pad
- Double-sided tape
- 15mm (5/8in) white, double-faced satin ribbon

1 Dowel and assemble the three tiers of the cake using royal icing (see Assembling Tiered Cakes).

2 Thinly roll out a long strip of dusky pink flower (petal/gum) paste so it is about 25–30cm (10–12in) long and 6–7cm (2½–2¾in) wide. Using the endless garret frill cutter, cut a scallop edge down one long side of the strip. Cut a straight edge parallel to the scalloped side using a sharp knife. The scalloped strip should now be approximately 2.5cm (1in) wide. Cover the strip with an acetate sheet to stop it from drying out.

3 Repeat this with the remaining dusky pink flower (petal/gum) paste until you have enough strips to fit round the base of the top and bottom tiers.

4 Working on one strip at a time, use the no. 3 piping tube (tip) to cut two small holes overlapping each other and side by side in each of the semi-circles along the scalloped edge. Using a small sharp knife, tease away a V-shape directly below the dots to form a cut-out heart shape. Repeat this down the scalloped edge on each strip of icing.

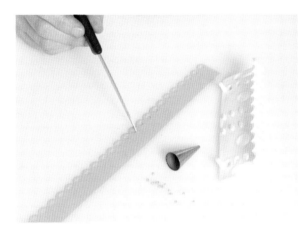

5 Brush edible glue around the base of the top tier and stick a scalloped piece of icing on to the cake with the straight edge at the base of the tier. Add another strip until you have gone around the tier and trim away the excess with a small sharp knife. Repeat this around the bottom tier.

6 Roll out some grey flower (petal/gum) paste until it is approximately 4mm (⅛in) thick. With a small sharp knife, cut thin strips about 4mm (⅛in) wide. Keeping them together, cut 4mm (⅛in) pieces across the strips to make small 'beads'. You will need 384 of these. Set aside to dry.

7 To make the rounded, elongated pearl-like beads, roll out thin sausages of ivory flower (petal/gum) paste until it is about 4mm (⅛in) thick and cut 4mm (⅛in) pieces with a small sharp knife. Roll each piece individually between your fingers to round the ends slightly. You will also 384 of these. Set aside to dry.

8 Thinly roll out some grey flower (petal/gum) paste and cut out oval shapes by placing an oval template (see Templates) on the paste, then cutting it out using the smaller circle cutter. Use a dusting brush to dust the shapes with edible silver dust. You will need 48 of these shapes in total. Cover with an acetate sheet.

9 To decorate the oval pieces, brush some edible glue on eight of them. Using tweezers, stick a pearl dragee in the centre of each one then surround them with small silver dragees. Next add the larger silver dragees on either side of these at the longest points. Smear on some more glue if necessary and add the flower (petal/gum) paste grey beads down the sides of the oval, and the oblong ivory flower (petal/gum) beads at the top and bottom. Finally, add a pearl dragee at the top and bottom of the oval and fill in the gaps with opal coarse sugar sprinkles. Cover the ovals with an acetate sheet while you work on the next eight, and so on.

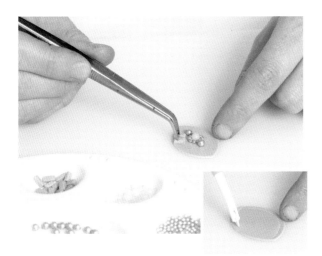

10 Thinly roll out some more grey flower (petal/gum) paste and cut out more pointed oval shapes, this time 2mm (1/16in) larger all around. Run a stitching tool around the outside of each shape and brush with edible silver dust using a dusting brush. You will need 48 of these shapes. Stick the smaller decorated ovals into the centre of each one.

11 Measure and mark 24 points around the cake at equal distances apart. The best way to do this is by marking opposite sides, then half way between these, then two points between each quarter. Stick the jewelled pieces to the cake, starting at the bottom and working upwards, using edible glue. The pieces should come up to the top of the cake.

TIP

Make all the beads you need for the cake in advance so you can concentrate on decorating the cake.

12 To make the flower on the top, use white florist tape to tape together a half-bunch of large pearl-head stamen.

13 To make the petals, roll out ivory flower (petal/gum) paste on a grooved board, leaving a thick ridge down the centre for the wire. Cut out a petal with the smaller peony petal cutter and insert a piece of wire into the base. Press the petal into the veiner, place it back on the board and run the veining tool back and forth across the top edge to make it frilly. Set aside to dry in a shallow cupped mould or apple tray. Make six petals using the smaller cutter and nine using the larger cutter.

14 Tape the six smaller petals around the stamen and add six larger petals in between them. The remaining petals can be taped on where required to add volume. Trim the end of the bounded wire with pliers and insert into a flower pick.

15 Finally, assemble the flower on top of the cake and then attach a length of satin ribbon around the cake board, securing with double-sided tape.

Jewelled cupcakes

These delightful, sparkly silver cupcakes would make charming gifts for wedding guests. They are decorated with circles of piped beading, as for the main cake.

Using edible glue, stick an edible diamond into the centre of the cupcake, and surround this with a circle of silver dragees. Brush a band of glue around the outside of the cupcake about 6mm (¼in) wide and sprinkle on some white coarse sugar sprinkles. Shake off the excess. Brush on some more glue inside the band and stick on a row of grey flower (petal/gum) paste beads. Next, stick on a row of grey beads alternating with pearl dragees. Then stick on a row of ivory flower (petal/gum) paste beads. Brush the remaining gap with more edible glue and sprinkle on white coarse sugar sprinkles. Shake off the excess.

YOU'LL ALSO NEED
* Cupcakes (flavour of choice) baked in silver cases and covered with very pale pink sugarpaste (rolled fondant)
* Edible diamonds
* White coarse sugar sprinkles

Butterfly gem cookies

YOU'LL ALSO NEED

❖ Butterfly-shaped
  vanilla cookies

❖ Grey royal icing

❖ Ivory royal icing

❖ Piping (pastry) bags

❖ No. 1.5 piping
  tube (tip)

❖ Grey and white
  coarse sugar
  sprinkles

These stylish butterfly cookies with their silver-edged wing tips would look very pretty on a silver platter on the wedding table; alternatively they could be packed into cellophane bags and tied with a silver bow as a gift for guests. They are iced with white and grey royal icing and decorated with dragees, beads and sugar sprinkles.

Outline the butterfly with soft-peak grey royal icing using a piping (pastry) bag with a no. 1.5 tube (tip). Pipe another line inside the outline leaving a 6mm (¼in) gap, which comes to a close at each end of the butterfly's wings. Flood the gap with thinned-down grey royal icing (see Royal-Iced Cookies) and immediately shake over some grey coarse sugar sprinkles so they stick into the wet icing. Shake off the excess and set aside to dry. Flood the inside of the wing with ivory royal icing (see Royal-Iced Cookies). Once the icing is dry, pipe a ball on the head and a large teardrop on the body and sprinkle with white coarse sugar sprinkles. Shake off the excess. Decorate with beads and pearls, securing them in place with edible glue.

PAINTING WITH FLOWERS

Weddings are often themed around the colours and varieties of flowers of the season. The start of the summer welcomes the most beautiful array of blues and purples including delphiniums, sweet peas, cornflowers and scabious, my chosen flower for this chapter.

The beautiful scabious flower grows naturally in the wild and I wanted to create a cake design that reflected this. This cake would complement perfectly the scabious bridal bouquet made by the amazing florist, Zita Elze, who has supplied all the flower arrangements in this book and gets it just right each time.

"A beautiful and relaxed cake design, ideal for a country wedding in summer"

Scabious cake

The delicate bluey-purple scabious flowers are quite fiddly to make but the end result is delightful. Each petal is individually shaped and attached to the centre before dusting. I adapted this flower from one in Alison Procter's book, *Simplifying Sugar Flowers*. The painted design around the base of each tier is very easy to do and really effective. You can also easily adapt this design using different colours.

MATERIALS

❖ One 10cm (4in) round cake, one 15cm (6in) round cake, one 20cm (8in) round cake, all 12cm (4½in) deep, prepared and iced with sugarpaste (rolled fondant) at least 12–24 hours in advance (see Covering Cakes)

❖ One 30cm (12in) round cake board, covered with white sugarpaste (rolled fondant) at least 12–24 hours in advance (see Icing Cake Boards)

❖ 250g (9oz) flower (petal/gum) paste

❖ Paste food colourings: Christmas green, spruce green, purple, baby blue

❖ Edible glue

❖ Dust colours: blue, purple

❖ Quarter quantity of royal icing

EQUIPMENT

❖ 6 hollow pieces of dowel cut to size (see Assembling Tiered Cakes)

❖ 3cm (1¼in) daisy cutter

❖ Paint palette

❖ Lobelia cutter, size 672 (Tinkertech)

❖ Acetate sheet

❖ Foam pad

❖ Ball tool

❖ Cocktail stick (toothpick)

❖ Small dusting brush

❖ Tweezers

❖ Icing smoother

❖ Small piping (pastry) bags and no. 1.5 piping tube (tip)

❖ 15mm (⅝in) white, double-faced satin ribbon

❖ Double-sided tape

1 Dowel and assemble the three tiers of the cake (see Assembling Tiered Cakes).

2 Colour approximately 50g (1³/₄oz) flower (petal/gum) paste with Christmas green paste food colouring and roll it out until it is about 1–2mm (¹/₁₆in) thick. Cut out daisy shapes using the cutter and set these aside until completely dry. You will need about 16 daisy shapes.

3 Put a small amount of spruce green paste food colouring into a paint palette and thin down with water using a no. 2 paintbrush. Carefully start painting the grass on to the cake tiers, making upward strokes from the base of each tier to about 4–5cm (1½–2in) up the side of the cake. Keep the paint fairly diluted so the grass is still quite subtle at this stage. Make some strokes slightly angled to each side and make them slightly different lengths.

4 Once you have gone around the cake on each tier, go over the grass again, making thinner strokes with a no. 1 paintbrush and using a less diluted paint to produce a stronger colour of green. Repeat this around each tier. Then stick dots of diluted purple and blue-coloured flower (petal/gum) paste in and among the grass to create little flowers.

5 Once the daisy-shaped pieces of paste are dry, roll small pea-sized balls of green flower (petal/gum) paste and flatten them slightly before sticking one into the centre of each daisy with a small amount of edible glue.

6 Colour approximately 175g (6oz) of the flower (petal/gum) paste with blue and purple paste food colouring. Roll out a small amount of the paste until it is about 1–2mm (¹/₁₆in) thick. Use the lobelia cutter to cut out 16, 24 or 32 petals (8 petals per flower). Cover the petals with an acetate sheet while you work on one or two petals at a time.

7 Use a small sharp knife to nip off the pointed ends of the petals so they are more rounded. Place the petal on to a foam pad and soften it slightly with the ball tool. Place the petal back on the non-stick board and frill the edges with a cocktail stick (toothpick), rolling it back and forth as you go over it.

TIP

Instead of painting the flowers, add tiny balls of blue and purple royal icing for extra texture.

8 Fold over the end opposite the frilled petals and stick the sides together with edible glue to form a pocket. Poke a cocktail stick (toothpick) into the pocket and lift the centre slightly. Trim the corners at the base of the pocket and cup the sides of the petal inwards before attaching them to the centre of the flower using a cocktail stick (toothpick) or the end of a paintbrush to help you. Secure in place with edible glue. You will need 8 petals per flower and approximately 16 flowers for the cake.

9 Roll long thin sausages of green flower (petal/gum) paste about 1–2mm (1/16in) thick and cut off tiny pieces using a small sharp knife. Working quickly, roll each piece around in your hand to make tiny balls. Set aside to dry.

10 When the petals are all assembled around the flowers, use a dusting brush to dust them with blue and purple powder, taking care not to break the fragile petals.

11 Make a paste by thinning down some of the green flower (petal/gum) paste with water and smear it in the centre of each flower with a paintbrush. Using tweezers to help you, stick the tiny balls on to the wet paste to create the centre of the flower.

12 Add any leftover green flower (petal/gum) paste to the remaining white flower (petal/gum) paste with some spruce green paste food colouring. Darken the paste for the flower stems. Add a touch more Christmas green paste if necessary. Roll small pieces of the paste out into long thin sausage shapes about the depth of the cake tiers. Use an icing smoother to help you roll them evenly. Trim the sausage shapes at one end.

13 Carefully paint a thin line of glue up the cake in a slight curve when the stems are going to go and attach the green paste to the cake, trimming it at the top with a small sharp knife.

14 Fill a piping (pastry) bag white royal icing and pipe a bead of icing to the flower head to stick it to the top of the stem. Repeat this around the cake on each tier until you have stuck on all the flowers.

15 Finish by piping a small snail trail border around the cake tiers using a no.1.5 piping tube (tip) (see Piping with Royal Icing). Finally, wrap a length of satin ribbon around the base board, and secure with double-sided tape.

Purple flower mini cakes

This pretty simplified version of the main cake design is perfect for a small cake, especially if you are planning to make quite a few of them. You will only need two or three scabious flowers for each cake. Serve either on individual plates or display several together on a tiered cake stand.

Thinly roll out some purply-blue flower (petal/gum) paste and cut out blossom shapes using the two sizes of cutters. You will need two smaller and two larger shapes per cake. Place the cut-out blossoms on a foam pad and soften the edges with a ball tool. Stick the smaller blossoms inside the larger blossoms and set aside to dry in some crumpled foil so the flower holds its shape. Roll and flatten a ball for the centre as described in the main project and pipe small dots of green royal icing into the centre. Roll the stems, paint around the base of the cake and attach the flowers as described in the main project.

Scabious cupcakes

These dainty cupcakes are dipped in white fondant and decorated with a single scabious flower. Serve on blue-flowered china plates for a mouthwatering and pretty treat.

Make the scabious flowers as described in the main project. Attach one flower to the top of each cupcake using a small amount of royal icing and pipe small dots of green royal icing into the centre.

YOU'LL ALSO NEED

❖ Cupcakes baked in silver cases (flavour of choice) and dipped in white fondant (see Fondant-Dipped Cupcakes)

BORDEAUX DRESS

I was really excited when one of my clients gave me a swatch from this stunning and unique Caroline Castigliano dress and asked me to use it as inspiration for their wedding cake. With its intricate white-on-ivory embroidery and beautiful appliqué, the dress is pure understated elegance.

It was a challenge to create the same effect with a wedding cake. However, I have taken the main elements from the material, simplified them slightly and recreated them in sugar using a variety of appliqué, embroidery and stitching techniques.

"White on ivory makes for a wedding cake that is both traditional and contemporary"

Lace wedding cake

The gaps between the tiers mimic the dress by allowing the jagged icing to hang down below the edge of the cake. The rest of the design is created mainly by using the zigzag and castellated strip cutters, the stitching tool and a daisy cutter.

MATERIALS

❖ One 18cm (7in) round cake, one 23cm (9in) round cake and one 30cm (12in) round cake, each 10cm (4in) deep, prepared and iced in ivory sugarpaste (rolled fondant) at least 12–24 hours in advance (see Baking and Covering Techniques)

❖ One 25cm (10in) round cake, 9cm (3½in) deep

❖ One 38cm (15in) round cake board, covered with ivory sugarpaste (rolled fondant) (see Icing Cake Boards)

❖ Half quantity of royal icing

❖ 600g (1lb 5oz) white flower (petal/gum) paste

❖ Edible glue

❖ Paste food colouring: brown

❖ Sugar crystals

EQUIPMENT

❖ Two 10cm (4in) round cake boards

❖ Two 20cm (8in) round cake boards

❖ 2.5cm (1in) ivory/bridal white satin ribbon

❖ Double-sided tape

❖ 10 hollow pieces of dowel cut to size (see Assembling Tiered Cakes)

❖ Zigzag and castellated strip cutters (FMM)

❖ Stitching tool

❖ Foam pad

❖ Boning tool

❖ Cutting wheel

❖ Medium oak leaf cutter

❖ Small and medium-sized daisy cutters

❖ Small piping (pastry) bag and nos. 1 and 2 piping tubes (tips)

❖ 15mm (5/8in) ivory/white, double-faced satin ribbon

1 Stick the two 10cm (4in) cake boards together with some royal icing. Repeat for the two 20cm (8in) boards. Wrap a length of 2.5cm (1in) ribbon twice round the boards and secure with double-sided tape.

2 Dowel the bottom and middle two tiers of the cake (see Assembling Tiered Cakes).

3 Stick the 30cm (12in) tier on to the centre of the base cake board with some royal icing. Stick the 20cm (8in) boards on top of this cake before stacking the 23cm (9in) and 18cm (7in) cakes on top (see Assembling Tiered Cakes). Stick the 10cm (4in) boards on the 18cm (7in) cake before assembling the top tier.

4 Roll out a long strip of white flower (petal/gum) paste approximately 3cm (1¼in) wide. Try to make the strip as long as possible without it becoming too difficult to work with (approximately 30cm (12in) is ideal). Using the zigzag strip cutter, cut along the icing and remove the excess paste. Using a large sharp knife, cut a neat edge down the opposite side. Run the stitching tool all the way down the strip about 3–4mm (⅛in) in from the straight edge.

5 With a small sharp knife, cut indentations along the zigzag edge. Place the strip on a foam pad and, using the boning tool, press and pull back along each triangular shape to make it curl upwards slightly.

TIP

Cover any cut flower (petal/gum) paste that you are not using with cling film (plastic wrap) or acetate sheets to prevent it from drying out too much.

6 Using a paintbrush and edible glue, stick the strip around the bottom edge of the top tier so that it hangs below the bottom of the cake. You will need to cut enough strips to go around both this tier and the 20cm (8in) tier. Ensure that you trim the strips so that they butt up to each other neatly and the zigzag edge carries on from one piece to the next.

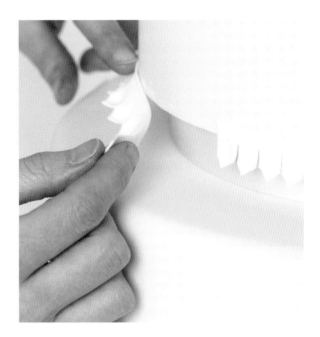

7 Roll out some more strips of flower (petal/gum) paste approximately 7.5cm (3in) wide and this time cut a castellated strip edge with the other cutter. Trim both ends neatly after five battlement shapes. Run round the whole piece with the stitching tool approximately 2mm (1/16in) in from the edge. Repeat to make four more strips. Then make five smaller strips, each with three battlement shapes. Stick these strips randomly around the cake tiers with edible glue, making them curve round in a semi-circular shape.

8 Complete the semi-circles on the top and 20cm (8in) tiers with a zigzag design made in the same way as for the trim around the base (see steps 4 and 5). Simply cut the zigzag strips to fit and trim the ends where they meet. You might need to cut single zigzag pieces to make the design fit together.

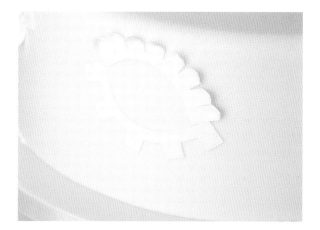

9 Make some more zigzag-edged shapes but this time cut the straight edge so it tapers in slightly at one end. Stick these to the cake in a random but even fashion with a small amount of edible glue.

10 The rest of the appliqué decoration is done by cutting long thin strips, small plain leaves and oak leaf shapes from thinly rolled-out flower (petal/gum) paste, using a large sharp knife, cutting wheel and leaf cutter. Use the stitching tool to mark the stitching pattern. The leaves are softened slightly using the boning tool on the foam pad as before. Stick the pieces on to the cake, filling in any empty spaces.

11 Cut out the daisies and run the stitching tool across the flower from each petal to the opposite side. Place them on the foam pad to curl the petals upwards slightly, as described in step 5, and stick them on to the cake. To make each daisy centre, colour a small amount of flower (petal/gum) paste pale brown using paste food colouring and roll it into a pea-sized ball. Flatten this slightly and press it into some sugar crystals. Stick the ball into the centre of the flowers.

12 Place a no. 1 piping tube (tip) in a small piping (pastry) bag, fill it with royal icing and roughly pipe leaves and vines in and among the appliqué pattern.

13 Place a no. 2 piping tube in a small piping (pastry) bag, fill it with royal icing and pipe a snail trail border (see Piping with Royal Icing) around the base of the 18cm (7in) and 30cm (12in) tiers. Finish by wrapping a length of ivory/white satin ribbon around the base board and secure with double-sided tape.

Appliqué lace mini cakes

Take elements from the main cake design to decorate these gorgeous miniature cakes. The little flowers sit really nicely on a small cake and the jagged edge around the bottom is an interesting and unique alternative to plain ribbon.

Make zigzag strips from flower (petal/gum) paste in the same way as for the main project to wrap around the bottom of the cake. Cut, shape, make and stick on the daisies as described in the main project. Finish by piping rough vines and leaves in and among the flowers.

YOU'LL ALSO NEED
❧ 5cm (2in) round miniature cakes iced in ivory sugarpaste (rolled fondant) (see Miniature Cakes)

Dress cookies

Make cookies to match the dress for a perfect favour or bridal party gift for the girls. Cut out the shape using your own template to make the design even more personalised.

Outline and flood the cookie with ivory coloured royal icing (see Royal-Iced Cookies). Place a no. 1 piping tube (tip) in a small piping (pastry) bag and fill it with white royal icing. Pipe the detail on the cookie to make lines, tiny zigzags and tear-drop shapes.

HERE COMES THE GROOM!

Wedding cakes don't always have to be about flowers and lace. This fabulous groom's cake eschews traditional floral decoration in favour of pleats, folds and embossing, all in the style of the groom's outfit. Groom cakes are becoming more and more popular and, with the increase in civil partnership celebrations, a groom's cake would make the perfect centrepiece.

The colour scheme for a groom's cake is classic grey, white and black, to reflect the formal wedding outfit. The pièce de résistance of the cake has to be the top tier – the ultimate top hat!

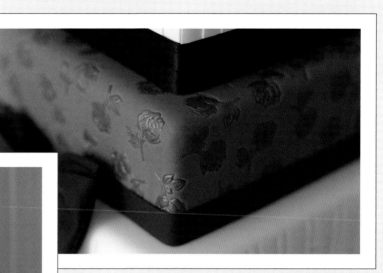

"An immaculately attired cake adds a sense of refinement to any wedding table"

Groom's cake

This eye-catching cake design is made using strips of icing and embossing, with some moulding for the bow tie. As the colours of the cake are limited, the different-shaped tiers add extra interest. The overall effect, however, is achieved by clean lines and smooth icing, so make sure you take care when covering the cake tiers.

MATERIALS

❖ One 13cm (5in) round cake, 13cm (5in) deep, tapered at the bottom to 10cm (4in) (see Carving and Sculpting Cakes), covered in grey sugarpaste (rolled fondant)

❖ One 15cm (6in) square cake, 13cm (5in) deep, prepared and iced with white sugarpaste (rolled fondant) (see Covering Cakes)

❖ One 20cm (8in) square cake, 7.5cm (3in) deep and one 25cm (10in) square cake, 14cm (5½in) deep, both layered, coated and refrigerated (see Layering, Filling and Preparation)

❖ One 35cm (14in) square cake board, covered with black sugarpaste (rolled fondant) at least 12–24 hours in advance (see Icing Cake Boards)

❖ One 18cm (7in) round, thin cake board, covered with grey sugarpaste (rolled fondant) at least 12–24 hours in advance (see Icing Cake Boards)

❖ 2kg (4lb 7oz) white sugarpaste (rolled fondant)

❖ Quarter quantity of royal icing

❖ 1kg (2lb 3½oz) grey sugarpaste (rolled fondant)

❖ Edible dust: silver

❖ Clear alcohol

❖ 250g (9oz) white flower (petal/gum) paste

❖ Edible glue

❖ 250g (9oz) black flower (petal/gum) paste

❖ Paste food colouring: black

EQUIPMENT

❖ Plastic spacer

❖ Ruler

❖ 11 hollow pieces of dowel cut to size (see Assembling Tiered Cakes)

❖ Rose embosser (Patchwork Cutters)

❖ 15mm (5/8in) black, double-faced satin ribbon

❖ Double-sided tape

❖ 6mm (¼in) black, grosgrain or double-faced satin ribbon

❖ Plain paper

1 Cover the 25cm (10in) cake with white sugarpaste (rolled fondant) (see Covering with Marzipan and Sugarpaste). Stick the cake on to the centre of the 35cm (14in) black-iced cake board with some royal icing. Using the spacer and a ruler to measure, mark vertical lines around the cake 15mm (5/8in) apart. You need to do this while the icing is still soft.

2 Dowel the 25cm (10in) tier before covering the 20cm (8in) square cake with grey sugarpaste (rolled fondant) (see Square Cakes). Dowel the 20cm (8in) tier and stack it on top of the 25cm (10in) cake (see Assembling Tiered Cakes).

3 Use the rose embosser to imprint a pattern in a random fashion all over the 20cm (8in) cake. Mix a little edible silver dust with clear alcohol and paint this over the rose indentations.

4 Assemble the 15cm (6in) tier on top of the 20cm (8in) tier and secure in place with royal icing.

5 Wrap three layers of 15mm (5/8in) black satin ribbon around the bottom of the 15cm (6in) cake. Wrap the first layer about 2.5cm (1in) up the side of the cake, the next layer below this and the final layer on top of these and flush with the bottom of the cake. Secure with double-sided tape.

6 Thinly roll out a large piece of white flower (petal/gum) paste and cut several 2.5cm (1in) wide strips at least 15cm (6in) long using a large sharp knife. You will need ten pieces plus a central piece for each side of the cake. Trim one end of each strip. Start by placing a strip vertically at each end of one side of the cake. Stick them in place with a small amount of edible glue and trim them neatly at the top of the cake with a small sharp knife. You will also need to trim the pieces at the corners slightly on the diagonal so they meet and sit neatly together.

7 Stick four more strips on each side of the cake so that they overlap each other as they come in towards the centre. Finish by placing one final strip in the centre. Trim the strips at the top of the cake as you go. Repeat this process for the remaining three sides of the 15cm (6in) tier.

8 To make the bow tie, first roll out some black flower (petal/gum) paste and cut a large strip approximately 25cm (10in) long and 6–7cm (2½–2¾in) wide. Pinch the strip in the centre. Pick up one end and make a pleat in the centre, then fold the two sides down in a concertina fashion before attaching them to the centre of the strip and securing in place with edible glue. Repeat this for the other side of the strip.

9 Repeat step 8 and make another bow but this time slightly longer and narrower. Stick this bow on top of the first bow with some edible glue.

10 Cut a strip 7cm (2¾in) long and 4cm (1½in) wide from some more thinly rolled-out black flower (petal/gum) paste. Fold the two sides over along the length of the strip and wrap the strip around the centre of both bows to create the knot. Secure in place with edible glue. Set aside to dry completely.

11 Roll another long, thin piece of black flower (petal/gum) paste for the strip around the bottom of the 20cm (8in) tier. You will probably need to do this in two stages. Cut the strips so they are 2cm (¾in) wide and trim them so they join each other neatly. Secure in place with edible glue.

12 Stick the grey, tapered 13cm (5in) top tier on to the round, grey-iced board using royal icing. Wrap a length of 15mm (⁵/₈in) black satin ribbon around the base of the cake and black grosgrain ribbon around the edge of the board. Dowel the 15cm (6in) tier and stick the top hat on top with royal icing.

TIP

You can emboss the stripes and rose pattern on to the cake before you stack the tiers but they will need to dry for at least 12 hours before assembling.

---

13 Make a triangular template from plain paper for the black jacket pieces around the bottom tier (see Templates). Thinly roll out some black flower (petal/gum) paste and use the template to cut out the shapes. Turn the template over to get a symmetrical triangle for the other side. Stick the pieces on to the cake with edible glue, joining them neatly together at the corners.

14 Colour a small amount of royal icing with black paste food colouring and use it to stick the bow on to the ledge between the 20cm (8in) and 25cm (10in) cake tiers.

15 Finish by securing a length of black satin ribbon around the base cake board, securing with double-sided tape.

Tuxedo cupcakes

These mini cupcakes, designed to enhance the stylish groom cake, will bring a smile to your guests' faces. Try varying the colour of the bow tie on each cake to add a sense of mischief to the day.

Thinly roll out some black flower (petal/gum) paste and cut out a circle with the circle cutter. Place the circle lightly over the cupcake to judge where to cut out the V shape for the jacket. Mark this with a sharp knife before cutting it off the cupcake. Stick the two pieces back on to the cupcake, securing them with edible glue. Cut the lapels in the same way, measuring them and marking the pieces on the cupcake with a knife before cutting them out. Stick them on to the cupcake. Press a small amount of black flower (petal/gum) paste into the bow tie mould for the bow tie and cut small circles from thinly rolled-out flower (petal/gum) paste using a no. 4 piping tube (tip) to create the buttons.

YOU'LL ALSO NEED
- ✤ Cupcakes baked in black foil cases and dipped in white fondant (see Fondant-Dipped Cupcakes) or covered in sugarpaste (rolled fondant)
- ✤ Circle cutter the size of the circumference of the top of the cupcake
- ✤ Bow tie mould
- ✤ No. 4 piping tube (tip)

Bow tie cookies

These simple-to-make bow tie cookies make a lovely favour for the male guests. The detail is in the piping – take care to go slowly when piping to produce neat, clean lines.

Outline and flood the cookies with black royal icing (see Royal-Iced Cookies). When the icing is dry, pipe over the detail and outline around the bow (see Piping with Royal Icing).

<table>
<tr><td>YOU'LL ALSO NEED</td></tr>
<tr><td>❖ Cookies cut using bow tie template (see Templates)</td></tr>
<tr><td>❖ Black royal icing</td></tr>
</table>

SUNSET MACAROONS

Big colourful balloons make fabulous decorations for a
fun and more informal wedding and are the inspiration
behind the appealing projects in this chapter.

My recent love affair with macaroons made it easy to choose
this extremely appropriate decoration for a fun wedding,
as they too are seen as the less serious side of cake making.
Their light and crunchy but soft and chewy texture is so
irresistibly sweet you can't help yourself but have another.
The serried rows of macaroons in sunset shades are linked by
classic gold ribbon, making a simple yet effective design.

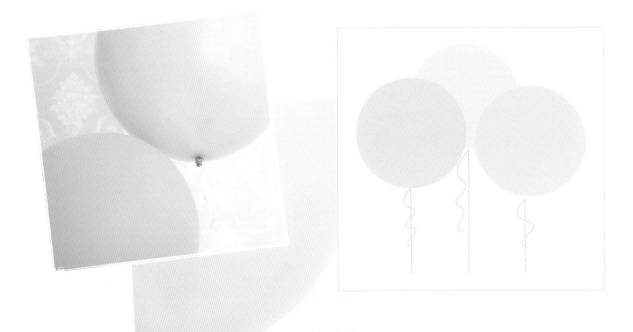

"This delightful cake brings together the elements of pure enjoyment and a touch of class"

Colourful macaroon cake

This colourful design is incredibly simple to achieve once you've mastered the art of making macaroons. I prefer to use the Italian meringue method, pouring hot sugar on to the whipped egg whites, as it tends to make a stiffer mixture that is easier to work with. All kinds of influences can affect how macaroons turn out – humid conditions and your oven in particular can cause problems – so be prepared to experiment and persevere if they don't turn out quite right on the first attempt.

MATERIALS

❖ One 13cm (5in) round cake, one 18cm (7in) round cake, one 23cm (9in) round cake and one 28cm (11in) round cake, each 10cm (4in) deep, prepared and iced in buttercup, peach, coral and pink sugarpaste (rolled fondant) at least 12–24 hours in advance (see Covering Cakes)

❖ One 35cm (14in) round cake board, covered with pink sugarpaste (rolled fondant) (see Icing Cake Boards)

❖ Half quantity of royal icing

❖ 480g (1lb 1oz) ground almonds

❖ 480g (1lb 1oz) icing sugar

❖ 360g (13oz) egg whites at room temperature

❖ 480g (1lb 1oz) caster sugar

❖ 120ml (4fl oz) water

❖ Paste food colouring: yellow, peach, coral, pink

❖ Half quantity of buttercream (frosting) (flavour of choice), at room temperature (see Fillings and Coverings)

EQUIPMENT

❖ 10 hollow dowels cut to size (see Assembling Tiered Cakes)

❖ One 10cm (4in) cake board, one 15cm (6in) cake board, one 20cm (8in) cake board and one 25cm (10in) cake board, each wrapped with 12mm (½in) gold ribbon

❖ Sieve

❖ Electric mixer with whisk attachment and mixing bowl

❖ Sugar (candy) thermometer

❖ Pastry brush

❖ Large spatula

❖ Large and medium-sized plastic piping (pastry) bags and piping tube (tip) with 8mm (¼in) hole

❖ Baking trays lined with greaseproof (wax) paper

❖ 15mm (5/8in) gold, double-faced satin ribbon

❖ Double-sided tape

1 Start by dowelling the bottom three tiers of the cake (see Assembling Tiered Cakes).

2 Stick the 25cm (10in) cake board on the centre of the 35cm (14in) iced cake board with some royal icing and then stack the 33cm (11in) tier on top. Repeat this for the remaining cake drums and tiers until the cake is all assembled, finishing with the smallest 10cm (4in) board and 13cm (5in) tier at the top.

3 Sift the ground almonds and icing sugar together into a large mixing bowl until you have a fine powder. You might need to do this twice.

TIP

Pulse the mixture in a food processor if the powder isn't fine enough.

4 Put half the egg whites (180g/6¹/₂oz) into the bowl of the electric mixer and start mixing on medium speed until the egg whites form soft peaks.

5 In the meantime, put the caster sugar and water into a saucepan and heat to 118°C (244°F) on a sugar (candy) thermometer. Pour the hot liquid steadily into the whipped egg whites with the mixer still going, taking care not to splatter it around the bowl. Keep the mixer going until the whites have cooled down completely and the mixture has become a smooth shiny meringue.

TIP

Brush the sides of the pan with water if the sugar starts to crystallize.

6 Pour the remaining unused egg whites on to the almond powder and stir briefly before tipping in half of the meringue mixture. Using a large spatula, carefully fold the mixture together in a figure-of-eight motion, and then add the rest of the meringue. It is better to slightly under-mix at this stage. Split the batter into four – you will need about half for the bottom tier, a quarter for the second tier, and the remaining quarter split between the top two tiers with slightly less for the smallest tier. Add the food colours to the mixtures so you have a yellow, a peach, a coral and a pink mixture. Do not over-mix the batter. The surface should be glossy and smooth.

7 Spoon one of the coloured mixtures into a large plastic piping (pastry) bag fitted with an 8mm (¼in) piping tube (tip). Pipe even-sized discs, about 2.5–3cm (1–1¼in) in diameter, on to baking trays lined with greaseproof (wax) paper, at least 3cm (1¼in) apart. Allow the uncooked macaroons to dry out for at least 20 minutes and form a skin. Preheat the oven to 150°C (300°F, Gas Mark 2) and bake the macaroons in the middle of the oven, one tray at a time for 10 to 12 minutes. After about 6 minutes the macaroons will lift up and little 'feet' will appear. They are ready when they are just firm to the touch.

8 Take the macaroons out of the oven and put the baking trays on a rack to cool for a few minutes. Remove the macaroons from the baking tray by carefully twisting them off or by running a small sharp knife underneath them. Set them aside or store in an airtight container until you need them. Repeat this for the different-coloured mixtures so you have enough macaroons (allowing for mishaps and any uneven-shaped ones).

9 Fill a medium-sized plastic piping (pastry) bag with some buttercream (frosting) and use it to stick the macaroon shells on to the cake, starting at the bottom of each tier and working upwards.

TIP

If the bottom of the cake is a bit untidy, wrap some ribbon around it (ideally the same colour as the icing) before sticking the macaroons on.

10 Finish by securing a length of 15mm (⅝in) gold, double-faced satin ribbon around the base board using double-sided tape.

Sunset polka dots

If you are short of time or are wary of attempting to make macaroons, you can achieve a similar design on your cake simply by sticking on circles cut from coloured icing.

Divide the flower (petal/gum) paste into three. Colour each piece separately with blush, peach and yellow paste food colouring. Dowel the 18cm (7in) tier and assemble the 10cm (4in) tier on top, securing it with some royal icing. Wrap a length of 15mm (⅝in) gold satin ribbon around the base of each tier and secure with double-sided tape. Thinly roll out the blush-coloured flower (petal/gum) paste and cut out enough circles to go around the base of both tiers. Using a paintbrush, stick the circles to the cake with a little edible glue. Repeat this with the peach and yellow flower (petal/gum) paste circles.

YOU'LL ALSO NEED

- ❖ One 10cm (4in) round cake and one 18cm (7in) round cake, each 10cm (4in) deep, iced in ivory sugarpaste (rolled fondant)
- ❖ Flower (petal/gum) paste
- ❖ 2cm (¾in) circle cutter
- ❖ Edible glue

Gold leaf macaroons

For a perfect treat to accompany the wedding cake, sandwich two macaroon shells together with a filling of your choice. Alternatively, serve them on their own for a luxurious tempting nibble.

Fill a plastic piping (pastry) bag with your choice of filling and pipe this on to one macaroon shell. Stick another macaroon shell of the same size on top. You will need to use enough filling to achieve a nice texture, but not so much that it becomes messy and sickly sweet. Decorate one side of each sandwiched macaroon with a flake of edible gold leaf to add a touch of class.

YOU'LL ALSO NEED
- ❧ 4–5cm (1½–2in) macaroon shells
- ❧ Filling of choice: buttercream (frosting), ganache or conserve
- ❧ Edible gold leaf

CLASSICAL CHARM

Every now and again when delivering a wedding cake, I discover the most gorgeous venue and No.11 Carlton House Terrace is one of these special places. The classical and intricate white wall panelling and plasterwork of its music room, offset against the soft ivories and shades of blue in the décor, offer the most beautiful backdrop for a wedding celebration and provide the inspiration behind these cake and cookie designs.

The combination of round and square tiers on this wedding cake echo the semi-circular and angled panels decorating the room while the Wedgwood blue icing really stands out against the white and ivory colour scheme.

"Elegant and beautiful, this classical wedding cake has a truly regal quality"

Panel cake

To achieve the symmetrical patterns, carefully trace the design on to greaseproof (wax) paper and mark out the design on the cake before piping. The swirl, scroll and fleur-de-lis motifs are created using 'pressure piping'; beads of icing are squeezed out and then the centres of these beads are dragged through to make teardrops and C- and S-shaped scrolls. When the icing is dry, it is painted with gold lustre to give it a really opulent look.

MATERIALS

❖ One 12.5cm (5in) round cake, one 23cm (9in) round cake, both 9cm (3½in) deep, prepared and iced in blue sugarpaste (rolled fondant) at least 12–24 hours in advance (see Covering Cakes)

❖ One 18cm (7in) round cake, one 28cm (11in) square cake, both 13cm (5in) deep, prepared and iced in blue sugarpaste (rolled fondant) at least 12–24 hours in advance (see Covering Cakes)

❖ One 35cm (14in) square cake, 9cm (3½in) deep, prepared and iced in blue sugarpaste (rolled fondant) at least 12–24 hours in advance (see Covering Cakes)

❖ One 40cm (16in) square, heavy duty cake board, or two cake drums stuck together with royal icing, covered with ivory sugarpaste (rolled fondant) (see Icing Cake Boards)

❖ White fat

❖ Half quantity of royal icing

❖ Paste food colourings: ivory/caramel and blue (I used baby blue and a touch of purple)

❖ Edible gold lustre

❖ Clear alcohol

EQUIPMENT

❖ 20 hollow pieces of dowel cut to size (see Assembling Tiered Cakes)

❖ Acetate sheet

❖ Small piping (pastry) bags and nos. 1, 1.5 and 2 piping tubes (tips)

❖ Semi-elliptic template (see Templates)

❖ Design template (see Templates)

❖ Greaseproof (wax) paper or baking parchment

❖ Measuring tape or ribbon

❖ 3–4 pins

❖ Needle scriber

❖ 15mm (5/8in) light blue, double-faced satin ribbon

❖ Double-sided tape

1 Start by dowelling and assembling the five tiers of the cake on top of the iced cake board (see Assembling Tiered Cakes).

2 Lightly grease a small piece of acetate with white fat. Fill a small piping (pastry) bag fitted with a no. 1.5 tube (tip) with caramel-coloured royal icing and pipe an outline using the semi-elliptic template (see Templates). Thin down 3 tablespoons of royal icing and flood the design (see 'Run-Out' Icing). You will need four of these decorations but it is best to always make a few spare ones to allow for any breakages. Set aside to dry completely.

3 Trace the design template on to greaseproof (wax) paper or baking parchment.

4 Use a measuring tape or ribbon to measure and mark with a needle scriber four points at equal distances apart around the 18cm (7in) cake tier. Hold the 18cm (7in) tier template against the cake. The centre of the template should be positioned on one of the marks. Hold the template in place with pins while you carefully prick the design on to the cake using the needle scriber, taking care not to press your fingers into the icing.

5 Mark the centre of each side of the 28cm (11in) square cake and carefully prick the design on to each side of the cake as before.

6 Fill three piping (pastry) bags fitted with nos. 1, 1.5 and 2 piping tubes (tips) with caramel-coloured royal icing and pipe the design on to the 18cm (7in) cake tier using the dotted design as your guide. All the piping work is created by piping various sizes of bead on to the cake and using the nozzle to drag through the icing to extend the shape. Squeeze harder and with a more constant pressure to make the elongated swirls. The larger shapes and scrolls and thicker lines are created using the no. 2 piping tube (tip) while the finer details are completed with the no.1 tube (tip).

TIP

If you find piping on to a stacked cake particularly hard, trace and pipe the design before assembling the cake, but take extra care not to knock the design when assembling the tiers on top of each other.

TIP

If you make a mistake, simply scrape off the icing with a small sharp knife and re-do it.

7 Pipe the design on to the 28cm (11in) tier as described in the previous step, leaving space for the run-out decoration and two little bows on either side of it (see Piping with Royal Icing).

8 For the decoration around the top tier, use a measuring tape to mark points approximately 5cm (2in) apart around the cake and 2.5cm (1in) up from the bottom. Pipe a dot on each mark and one in between, about 1cm (3/8in) below. Pipe small teardrops with a slight curve going from the lower dots to the upper dots in both directions.

9 Use a measuring tape to mark points approximately 2.5cm (1in) apart around the middle tier and about 2.5cm (1in) up from the base. Use a no. 2 piping tube (tip) to pipe the two largest curved teardrops, which should meet where you have marked the point. Repeat this around the cake. Use the no. 1.5 piping tube (tip) to pipe the teardrops and dots above and the dot at the bottom of the design.

10 Mark points about 2.5cm (1in) apart along the sides of the bottom tier and pipe the simple teardrop and dot design around the cake as described in the previous steps.

11 Carefully remove the run-out decoration from the acetate and attach it to the cake with royal icing. Pipe the little bows on either side of the decoration using the no.1 piping tube (tip) and make lots of little teardrop shapes. Pipe the 3 'drop' lines and dots on the run-out using the same piping tube (tip).

12 When the royal icing is dry, use a fine paintbrush to paint over the pattern on all five tiers with gold lustre mixed with clear alcohol.

13 Colour approximately 3 teaspoons of royal icing to match the colour of the sugarpaste (rolled fondant icing) and pipe a snail trail border around each tier (see Piping with Royal Icing).

14 Finish by securing a length of satin ribbon around the base board and secure it in place with double-sided tape.

Mini fleur-de-lis cakes

Choose simplified motifs from the main cake design to decorate these ornamental miniature cakes. Pipe the design around the sides of the cakes as well as on the top.

Mark the centre on each side of the square cakes or around the round cakes at equal distances to use as a guide to help you pipe an even pattern. You don't need to worry about templates for the smaller cakes. Pipe and paint the design as described in the main project.

YOU'LL ALSO NEED
❖ 5cm (2in) round and/or square miniature cakes, iced in blue sugarpaste (rolled fondant) (see Miniature Cakes)

Medallion cookies

Extend the classical theme by icing and decorating these simple cookies with piped scrolls and teardrops using caramel-coloured royal icing. Serve to guests at the end of the wedding feast.

Outline and flood each cookie with blue-coloured royal icing (see Royal-Iced Cookies). Pipe simple scrolls, teardrops and dots on the icing to match the main cake design. When the icing is dry, paint over the top with gold lustre, as described in the main project.

YOU'LL ALSO NEED
❖ Cookies cut using a 4cm (1½in) circle cutter

FLORA ABUNDANCE

Incorporating delicate embroidery and big textured and layered flowers, Claire Pettibone's fabulous Flora dress is one of my all-time favourite bridal gown designs. The use of colour in the design is unusual for a wedding gown but this is also what makes it unique.

This dress provided a marvellous inspiration for my floral wedding cake, allowing me to use two of my favourite decorations - bold flowers and twining stems. The square design, with its tiers of different depths, allows you to experiment with the placement of the flowers.

"*Make a statement with this gorgeous flowery creation, straight out of a fairytale*"

Flora wedding cake

A statement dress deserves nothing less than a lovely big cake to showcase its striking detail. Be bold in your decoration – this is not a design for the fainthearted. Paint the vines/leaves with edible platinum gold to resemble the metallic tinsel-like thread on the dress.

MATERIALS

❖ One 10cm (4in) square cake, 9cm (3½in) deep, one 15cm (6in) round cake, 10cm (4in) deep, one 20cm (8in) square cake, 15cm (6in) deep, one 23cm (10in) square cake, 10cm (4in) deep, and one 33cm (13in) square cake, 11cm (4¼in) deep, all prepared and iced in ivory sugarpaste (rolled fondant) at least 12–24 hours in advance (see Covering Cakes)

❖ One 40cm (16in) square, heavy duty cake board, or two cake drums stuck together with royal icing, covered with ivory sugarpaste (rolled fondant) (see Icing Cake Boards)

❖ 500g (1lb 1½oz) white flower (petal/gum) paste

❖ Paste food colourings: paprika, brown, dusky pink, baby blue, ivory

❖ Edible glue

❖ Silver dragees

❖ Half quantity of royal icing

❖ Clear alcohol

❖ Platinum gold dust (I mixed silver into gold)

EQUIPMENT

❖ 21 hollow pieces of dowel cut to size (see Assembling Tiered Cakes)

❖ 65mm (2⅝in) peony cutter

❖ Veining stick

❖ Shallow cupped mould or apple tray

❖ Small and medium-sized five-petal rose cutters (FMM)

❖ Multi-flower veiner

❖ Foam pad

❖ Ball tool

❖ Paint palette

❖ Small primrose cutter

❖ Small piping (pastry) bags and nos. 1, 1.5 and 2 piping tubes (tips)

❖ Circle cutter

❖ Foil

❖ 2.5cm (1in) ivory satin ribbon

❖ Double-sided tape

1 Start by dowelling and assembling all five tiers on the iced cake board (see Assembling Tiered Cakes).

2 To make the flowers, thinly roll out some white flower (petal/gum) paste and cut out petals using the peony cutter. You will need six of these to make up one flower. Vein the rounded end of each petal with a veining stick, carefully moving it back and forth over the flower (petal/gum) paste until it ripples up. Place the petals into a shallow cupped mould until they are nearly dry and can hold their shape.

3 Colour 200g (7oz) of the flower (petal/gum) paste with paprika and thinly roll out a portion of it. Using the large five-petal rose cutter, cut out the next layer of the flower. Use the outer V-shape from the cutter to make indentations on each petal and press the paste into the multi-flower veiner. Place the flower on to a foam pad and, using the ball tool, press lightly inside the edge of each petal to make it cup upwards slightly. Set aside to dry in a paint palette so it holds its shape. Repeat for the next layer of the flower using the small five-petal rose cutter.

4 To make the centre of the flower, cut a small primrose shape from the pale paprika-coloured paste. Place it on the foam pad and soften it slightly to give it some shape. Use a fine paintbrush to dab a small amount of edible glue in the centre of the tiny flower and attach a silver dragee. Set aside to dry.

5 Fill a small piping (pastry) bag fitted with a no. 1 tube (tip) with pale paprika-coloured royal icing and pipe an outline around all the five-petalled flowers.

6 Cut a small disc from some thinly rolled-out white flower (petal/gum) paste using the circle cutter. Arrange the outer white petals around the disc and secure them in place with a small amount of edible glue. Next stick the largest paprika-coloured flower followed by the smallest five-petal flowers into the centre and finish with the tiny primrose-shaped flower. Pipe tiny paprika-coloured dots of royal icing on the tips of the primrose and set the finished flower aside to dry completely.

TIP

Place the flower back in the shallow cupped mould or on some crumpled foil so it keeps its slightly cupped shape. You will need 16 to 18 flowers for this five-tier cake.

7 Repeat the process to make about 16 smaller five-petal flowers and primroses for the two-layer flowers on the cake. Set them aside to dry.

8 Colour approximately 3 tablespoons of royal icing with brown paste food colouring until you have a caramel colour. Fill a small piping (pastry) bag fitted with a no. 2 tube (tip) with this icing. Starting at the top of the cake, pipe the vines down and across each tier, thinking about where you are going to place the flowers. You will need to match up the vines on each side of the cake so arrange the cake on a slight angle to check this when you begin each side.

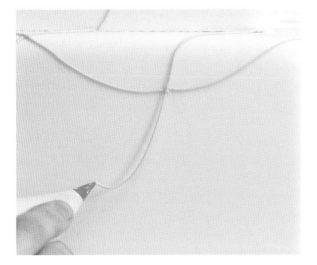

TIP

Tip the cake slightly to pipe the vines if you find they are breaking easily.

9 To create the leaves, pipe a leaf outline and drag the icing inwards and down to the vine using a damp paintbrush. Repeat this all the way down the vines on opposite sides.

10 Colour some more royal icing with dusky pink paste food colouring and fill a piping (pastry) bag fitted with a no. 2 tube (tip) with this icing. Use the brush embroidery technique as shown in step 9 to make the pink flowers. Pipe a blossom outline and drag the icing inwards with a damp paintbrush.

11 To make the small blue flowers, use baby blue-coloured royal icing in a piping (pastry) bag fitted with a no. 1.5 tube (tip) and pipe five little teardrops which meet together at the centre of the flower. Use a damp paintbrush to flatten the icing slightly. When dry, randomly pipe a few small dots of pink icing on top and dab it down again with a damp paintbrush.

12 Colour some more royal icing with ivory paste food colouring until it is the same colour as the cake. Pipe an ivory snail trail border (see Piping with Royal Icing) around the base of each cake tier.

13 Mix a few drops of clear alcohol into some platinum gold-coloured dust and use this to carefully paint the leaves and vines.

14 Finish by carefully sticking all the large handcrafted flowers on to the cake with some ivory-coloured royal icing. Wrap a length of 2.5cm (1in) ivory satin ribbon around the base board and secure in place with double-sided tape.

Floral fancies

Square fondant fancies are an ideal accompaniment to the main cake design. Here I have used the smaller handcrafted flowers from the main project to decorate the fancies but you could also decorate them using the brush embroidery technique.

Make several small flowers in ivory flower (petal/gum) paste as for the flowers for the main cake project (see steps 3-7 of main project). Stick one flower to each of the fancies with a small amount of ivory royal icing. Stick a silver dragee into the centre of each flower to complete.

YOU'LL ALSO NEED
* 4cm (1½in) square fondant fancies dipped in ivory fondant (see Fondant Fancies) and set in gold cases
* Ivory royal icing

Embroidered flower cookies

These incredibly pretty cookies are made using the same shape cutter as the sugar flowers on the main cake, and decorated with the same delicate brush embroidery design.

Roll out the ivory sugarpaste (rolled fondant) until it is about 3mm (1/8in) thick and cut out the flowers to match the shape of the cookie. Stick the sugarpaste (rolled fondant) on to the cookie using some boiled apricot masking spread or strained jam (jelly) (see Covering Cookies with Sugarpaste). Decorate the cookies using the same brush embroidery design as in the main project.

YOU'LL ALSO NEED
* Cookies cut using a large five-petal rose cutter (FMM) with V-shapes cut from each petal
* Ivory sugarpaste (rolled fondant)
* Apricot masking spread or strained jam (jelly)

*"The foundation of
an unforgettable cake"*

Recipes and techniques

CAKE RECIPES

It's important that your cake tastes as good as it looks. Always try to use the finest ingredients that you can find, as this will make a big difference to the flavour. In order to achieve a professional, crust-free result, bake your cake in a tin 2.5cm (1in) bigger than the actual size you would like your finished cake to be. The sizes and quantities specified in the charts on the following pages will make cakes about 9cm (3½in) deep. For shallower cakes, miniature cakes and fondant fancies, use smaller quantities (see Miniature Cakes and Fondant Fancies). For cakes 35cm (14in) or larger, you will need to join together four smaller cakes. Don't forget to bake slightly larger than the size required. For example, for a 35cm (14in) square cake, you would need to bake four 20cm (8in) squares or equivalent. For many of the projects you can use any of the cake recipes.

EQUIPMENT
FOR CAKE MAKING

❖ Greaseproof (wax) paper or baking parchment and tins
❖ Kitchen scales
❖ Measuring spoons and jug (pitcher)
❖ Large electric mixer
❖ 2–3 mixing bowls in different sizes
❖ Sieve (strainer)
❖ Spatula
❖ Palette knife
❖ Metal skewer
❖ Saucepan
❖ Large metal spoon
❖ Clingfilm (plastic wrap)

CLASSIC SPONGE CAKE

For a really light sponge cake, it is better to separate the mixture between two tins. If you want three layers for your cake, split the mixture one-third/two-thirds. For smaller cakes, you can also cut three layers of sponge from a larger square cake. For example, a 15cm (6in) round cake can be cut from a 30cm (12in) square cake (see opposite).

1 Preheat your oven to 160°C/325°F/Gas Mark 3 and line your tins (see Preparing Cake Tins).

2 In a large electric mixer, beat the butter and sugar together until light and fluffy. Add the eggs gradually, beating well between each addition, then add the flavouring.

TIP

Make sure that the butter and eggs you are using are at room temperature before you start.

3 Sift the flour, add to the mixture and mix very carefully until just combined.

4 Remove the mixing bowl from the mixer and fold the mixture through gently with a spatula to finish. Tip the mixture into your prepared tin or tins and spread with a palette knife or the back of a spoon.

5 Bake in the oven until a skewer inserted into the centre of your cakes comes out clean. The baking time will vary depending on your oven. Check small cakes after 20 minutes and larger cakes after 40 minutes.

6 Allow to cool, then wrap the cake well in clingfilm (plastic wrap) and refrigerate until ready to use.

If cutting three layers from a larger square cake: for a 15cm (6in) round cake, bake an 8-egg/400g (14oz) butter etc. mix in a 30cm (12in) square tin; for a 13cm (5in) round or square cake, bake a 7-egg/350g (12½oz) mix in a 28cm (11in) square tin; for a 10cm (4in) round or square cake, bake a 6-egg/300g (10½oz) mix in a 25cm (10in) square tin. For sculpted and carved cakes, add 10 per cent extra flour.

Deeper cakes

For deeper cakes, simply bake up to one and a half times the recipe. You might need to do this in two batches if you only have a couple of tins. Allow them to cool slightly before turning the cakes out and re-filling with the mixture.

Shelf life

Sponges should be made up to 24 hours in advance. Freeze the sponge if it is not being used the next day. After the 1-2 day process of layering and covering of the cakes, the finished cakes should last up to 3-4 days out of the fridge.

Cake size	13cm (5in) round / 10cm (4in) square	15cm (6in) round / 13cm (5in) square	18cm (7in) round / 15cm (6in) square	20cm (8in) round / 18cm (7in) square	23cm (9in) round / 20cm (8in) square	25cm (10in) round / 23cm (9in) square	28cm (11in) round / 25cm (10in) square	30cm (12in) round / 28cm (11in) square	33cm (13in) round / 30cm (12in) square
Unsalted butter	150g (5½oz)	200g (7oz)	250g (9oz)	325g (11½oz)	450g (1lb)	525g (1lb 2½oz)	625g (1lb 6oz)	800g (1lb 12oz)	1kg (2lb 3½oz)
Caster (superfine) sugar	150g (5½oz)	200g (7oz)	250g (9oz)	325g (11½oz)	450g (1lb)	525g (1lb 2½oz)	625g (1lb 6oz)	800g (1lb 12oz)	1kg (2lb 3½oz)
Medium eggs	3	4	5	6	9	10	12	14	17
Vanilla extract (tsp)	½	1	1	1½	2	2	2½	4	4½
Self-raising (-rising) flour	150g (5½oz)	200g (7oz)	250g (9oz)	325g (11½oz)	450g (1lb)	525g (1lb 2½oz)	625g (1lb 6oz)	800g (1lb 12oz)	1kg (2lb 3½oz)

CLASSIC CHOCOLATE CAKE

This chocolate cake recipe is really quick and easy to make and has a lovely light texture. You should split the cake mixture between two tins, either dividing it equally or into one-third and two-thirds for three-layered cakes. Use a chocolate ganache filling rather than buttercream (frosting) for a richer, more indulgent flavour (see Ganache).

1 Preheat your oven to 160°C/325°F/Gas Mark 3 and line your tins (see Preparing Cake Tins).

2 Sift the flour, cocoa powder (unsweetened cocoa) and baking powder together.

3 In a large electric mixer, beat the butter and sugar together until light and fluffy. Meanwhile, crack your eggs into a separate bowl.

4 Add the eggs to the mixture gradually, beating well between each addition.

5 Add half the dry ingredients and mix until just combined before adding half the milk. Repeat with the remaining ingredients. Mix until the mixture starts to come together.

6 Finish mixing the ingredients together by hand with a spatula, and spoon into your prepared tins.

7 Bake in the oven until a skewer inserted into the centre of your cakes comes out clean. The baking time will vary depending on your oven. Check smaller cakes after 20 minutes and larger cakes after 40 minutes.

8 Leave to cool, then wrap the cakes well in clingfilm (plastic wrap) and refrigerate until ready to use.

Deeper cakes

For deeper cakes, simply bake up to one and a half times the recipe. You might need to do this in two batches, if you only have a couple of tins. Allow them to cool slightly before turning the cakes out and re-filling with the mixture.

Shelf life

Chocolate cakes should be made up to 24 hours in advance. Freeze the cake if it is not being used the next day. After the 1-2 day process of layering and covering of the cakes, the finished chocolate cakes should last up to 3-4 days out of the fridge.

Cake size	13cm (5in) round / 10cm (4in) square	15cm (6in) round / 13cm (5in) square	18cm (7in) round / 15cm (6in) square	20cm (8in) round / 18cm (7in) square	23cm (9in) round / 20cm (8in) square	25cm (10in) round / 23cm (9in) square	28cm (11in) round / 25cm (10in) square	30cm (12in) round / 28cm (11in) square	33cm (13in) round / 30cm (12in) square
Plain (all-purpose) flour	170g (6oz)	225g (8oz)	280g (10oz)	365g (13oz)	500g (1lb 1½oz)	585g (1lb 4½oz)	700g (1lb 8½oz)	825g (1lb 13oz)	1kg (2lb 3½oz)
Cocoa powder (unsweetened cocoa)	30g (1oz)	40g (1½oz)	50g (1¾oz)	65g (2¼oz)	90g (3¼oz)	100g (3½oz)	125g (4½oz)	150g (5½oz)	185g (6½oz)
Baking powder (teaspoons)	1½	2	2½	3¼	4½	5¼	6¼	7½	9¼
Unsalted butter	150g (5½oz)	200g (7oz)	250g (9oz)	325g (11½oz)	450g (1lb)	525g (1lb 2½oz)	625g (1lb 6oz)	750g (1lb 10½oz)	925g (2lb ½oz)
Caster (superfine) sugar	130g (4½oz)	175g (6oz)	220g (8oz)	285g (10oz)	400g (14oz)	460g (1lb)	550g (1lb 3½oz)	650g (1lb 7oz)	800g (1lb 12oz)
Large eggs	2½	3	4	5	7	8½	10	12	15
Full-fat (whole) milk	100ml (3½fl oz)	135ml (4½fl oz)	170ml (5¾fl oz)	220ml 7½fl oz)	300ml 10¼fl oz)	350ml 11¾fl oz)	425ml 14½fl oz)	500ml 17fl oz)	600ml 20fl oz)

Additional flavourings

For the classic chocolate cake:

Orange Use the finely grated zest of 1 orange per 2 eggs.

Coffee liqueur Add 1 shot of cooled espresso coffee per 2–3 eggs and add coffee liqueur to taste to the sugar syrup (see Sugar Syrup).

Chocolate hazelnut Replace 10 per cent of the flour with the same quantity of ground hazelnuts and layer with chocolate hazelnut spread and ganache (see Ganache).

Additional flavourings

For the classic sponge cake:

Lemon Add the finely grated zest of 1 lemon per 100g (3½oz) sugar.

Orange Add the finely grated zest of 2 oranges per 250g (9oz) sugar.

Chocolate Replace 10g (¼oz) flour with 10g (¼oz) cocoa powder (unsweetened cocoa) per 100g (3½oz) flour.

Banana Replace the caster (superfine) sugar with brown sugar. Add 1 overripe, mashed banana and ½ teaspoon mixed spice (apple pie spice) per 100g (3½oz) flour.

CARROT CAKE

Grated carrot and chopped pecan nuts give this recipe a lovely texture as well as a divine taste. I prefer to have only two layers of carrot cake sandwiched together with one layer of buttercream (frosting) to make up one tier, so for the best results divide the quantities listed opposite between two tins to bake them. Lemon-flavoured buttercream (frosting) is my favourite choice of filling, as it complements the cake perfectly.

1 Preheat the oven to 160°C/325°F/Gas Mark 3 and line your tins (see Preparing Cake Tins).

2 In a large electric mixer, beat together the sugar and vegetable oil for about a minute until the mixture is well combined.

3 Crack your eggs into a bowl and add them to the mixture one at a time, beating well between each addition.

4 Sift together the dry ingredients and add them to the cake mixture, alternating with the grated carrot.

5 Fold in the chopped nuts.

6 Divide the mixture between two prepared tins and bake in the oven for 20–50 minutes, depending on size. Check that the cake is cooked by inserting a skewer into the centre, which should come out clean.

7 Leave to cool, then wrap the cakes well in clingfilm (plastic wrap) and refrigerate until ready to use.

Deeper cakes
For deeper cakes, simply bake up to one and a half times the recipe. You might need to do this in two batches, if you only have a couple of tins. Allow them to cool slightly before turning the cakes out and re-filling with the mixture.

TIP

You can replace the pecans with walnuts, hazelnuts or a mixture of nuts, if you prefer.

Shelf life

Carrot cakes should be made up to 24 hours in advance. Freeze the cake if it is not being used the next day. After the 1-2 day process of layering and covering of the cakes, the finished carrot cakes should last up to 3-4 days out of the fridge.

┌─ TIP

The carrot cake is very moist and not suitable for carved cakes, as it would just crumble away.

Cake size	13cm (5in) round 10cm (4in) square	15cm (6in) round 13cm (5in) square	18cm (7in) round 15cm (6in) square	20cm (8in) round 18cm (7in) square	23cm (9in) round 20cm (8in) square	25cm (10in) round 23cm (9in) square	28cm (11in) round 25cm (10in) square	30cm (12in) round 28cm (11in) square	33cm (13in) round 30cm (12in) square
Brown sugar	135g (4¾oz)	180g (6½oz)	250g (9oz)	320g (11½oz)	385g (13½oz)	525g (1lb 2½oz)	560g (1lb 4oz)	735g (1lb 10oz)	900g (2lb)
Vegetable oil	135ml (4½fl oz)	180ml (6fl oz)	250ml (8½fl oz)	320ml (10¾fl oz)	385ml (13fl oz)	525ml (18fl oz)	560ml (19fl oz)	735ml (25fl oz)	900ml (30½fl oz)
Medium eggs	2	2½	3	4	5	6½	7	9	11
Self-raising (-rising) flour	200g (7oz)	275g (9½oz)	375g (13oz)	480g (1lb 1oz)	590g (1lb 5oz)	775g (1lb 11½oz)	850g (1lb 14oz)	1.1kg (2lb 7oz)	1.35kg (3lb)
Mixed spice (apple pie spice) (tbsp)	1	1½	2	2½	3	4	4½	5½	5¾
Bicarbonate of soda (baking soda) (tsp)	¼	½	¾	¾	1	1	1¼	1½	2
Finely grated carrot	300g (10½oz)	385g (13½oz)	525g (1lb 2½oz)	675g (1lb 8oz)	825g (1lb 13oz)	1.05kg (2lb 5oz)	1.2kg (2lb 11oz)	1.5kg (3lb 5oz)	1.8kg (4lb)
Finely chopped pecans	65g (2¼oz)	85g (3oz)	120g (4¼oz)	150g (5½oz)	175g (6oz)	240g (8½oz)	270g (9½oz)	350g (12½oz)	425g (15oz)

TRADITIONAL FRUIT CAKE

I have made many fruit cake recipes over the years, and this is one of my favourite ones. You can replace the dried fruits with other dried fruits of your choice or keep it simple by using only pre-mixed dried fruit. Choose different types of alcohol to flavour your cake according to your own taste – I like to use equal quantities of cherry brandy and plain brandy. Rum, sherry and whisky also work well.

You need to soak your dried fruit and mixed peel in the alcohol at least 24 hours in advance. Ideally, your cake needs to be baked at least one month before it is to be eaten to allow it time to mature. You can also 'feed' your cake with alcohol once a week to keep the cake really moist and to enhance its flavour.

1 Preheat your oven to 150°C/300°F/Gas Mark 2 and line your tin with two layers of greaseproof (wax) paper or baking parchment for small cakes, and three layers for larger cakes (see Preparing Cake Tins).

2 In a large electric mixer, beat the butter and sugar together with the lemon and orange zest until fairly light and fluffy. Add the orange juice to the soaked fruit and mixed peel.

3 Gradually add your eggs, one at a time, beating well between each addition.

4 Sift the flour and spices together and add half the flour mixture together with half the soaked fruit mixture to the cake mixture. Mix until just combined and then add the remaining flour mixture and fruit mixture.

5 Gently fold in the almonds and treacle (molasses) with a large metal spoon until all the ingredients are combined and then spoon the mixture into your prepared baking tin.

6 Cover the top loosely with some more greaseproof (wax) paper or baking parchment and then bake in the oven for the time indicated or until a skewer inserted into the centre comes out clean.

7 Pour some more alcohol over the cake while it is hot and leave to cool in the tin.

8 Remove from the tin and wrap your cake in a layer of greaseproof (wax) paper and then foil to store.

Deeper cakes
Unfortunately, fruit cakes cannot be made any bigger than the height of the tin. If you need to give your fruit cake a little extra height, you can double-board it (place it on two cake boards stuck together with royal icing) or add a thicker layer of marzipan to the top of the cake before icing it. All fruit cakes are marzipanned before being iced.

Shelf life
Fruit cakes should be made at least 4-6 weeks before being eaten to allow enough time for them to mature. Fruit cakes can be kept up to 9 months or can be frozen to preserve their shelf life.

Cake size	10cm (4in) round	13cm (5in) round / 10cm (4in) square	15cm (6in) round / 13cm (5in) square	18cm (7in) round / 15cm (6in) square	20cm (8in) round / 18cm (7in) square	23cm (9in) round / 20cm (8in) square	25cm (10in) round / 23cm (9in) square	28cm (11in) round / 25cm (10in) square	30cm (12in) round / 28cm (11in) square	33cm (13in) round / 35cm (14in) square
Currants	100g (3½oz)	125g (4½oz)	175g (6oz)	225g (8oz)	300g (10½oz)	375g (13oz)	450g (1lb)	550g (1lb 3½oz)	660g (1lb 7½oz)	875g (1lb 15½oz)
Raisins	125g (4½oz)	150g (5½oz)	200g (7oz)	275g (9½oz)	350g (12½oz)	450g (1lb)	555g (1lb	675g (1lb 8oz)	800g (1lb 12oz)	1kg (2lb 3½oz)
Sultanas (golden raisins)	125g (4½oz)	150g (5½oz)	200g (7oz)	275g (9½oz)	350g (12½oz)	450g (1lb)	555g (1lb	675g (1lb 8oz)	800g (1lb 12oz)	1kg (2lb 3½oz)
Glacé (candied) cherries	40g (1½oz)	50g (1¾oz)	70g (2½oz)	100g (3½oz)	125g (4½oz)	150g (5½oz)	180g (6½oz)	200g (7oz)	250g (9oz)	330g (12oz)
Mixed peel	25g (1oz)	30g (1oz)	45g (1½oz)	50g (1¾oz)	70g (2½oz)	85g (3oz)	110g (4oz)	125g (4½oz)	150g (5½oz)	195g (7oz)
Cherry brandy and brandy mix (tbsp)	2	2½	3	3½	5	6	7	8	9	13
Slightly salted butter	100g (3½oz)	125g (4½oz)	175g (6oz)	225g (8oz)	350g (12½oz)	375g (13oz)	450g (1lb)	550g (1lb 3½oz)	660g (1lb 7½oz)	875g (1lb 15½oz)
Brown sugar	100g (3½oz)	125g (4½oz)	175g (6oz)	225g (8oz)	350g (12½oz)	375g (13oz)	450g (1lb)	550g (1lb 3½oz)	660g (1lb 7½oz)	875g (1lb 15½oz)
Grated zest of lemon (per fruit)	¼	½	¾	1	1½	2	2	2½	3	4
Grated zest of small orange (per fruit)	¼	½	¾	1	1½	2	2	2½	3	4
Juice of small orange (per fruit)	¼	¼	½	½	¾	¾	1	1½	1½	2
Medium eggs	2	2½	3	4½	6	7	8½	10	12	16
Plain (all-purpose) flour	100g (3½oz)	125g (4½oz)	175g (6oz)	225g (8oz)	350g (12½oz)	375g (13oz)	450g (1lb)	550g (1lb 3½oz)	660g (1lb 7½oz)	875g (1lb 15½oz)
Mixed spice (apple pie spice) (tsp)	½	½	¾	¾	1	1¼	1½	1½	1¾	2½
Ground nutmeg (tsp)	¼	¼	½	½	½	¾	¾	1	1	1½
Ground almonds	10g (¼oz)	15g (½oz)	20g (¾oz)	25g (1oz)	35g (1¼oz)	45g (1½oz)	55g (2oz)	65g (2¼oz)	75g (2¾oz)	100g (3½oz)
Flaked (slivered) almonds	10g (¼oz)	15g (½oz)	20g (¾oz)	25g (1oz)	35g (1¼oz)	45g (1½oz)	55g (2oz)	65g (2¼oz)	75g (2¾oz)	100g (3½oz)
Black treacle (molasses) (tbsp)	½	¾	1	1½	1½	1¾	2	2½	3	4
Baking time (hours)	2½	2¾	3	3½	4	4½	4¾	5½	6	7

FILLINGS & COVERINGS

Fillings are used to add flavour and moisture to a cake and should complement the sponge mixture. Buttercream (frosting) and flavoured ganache are the two most widely used fillings and both recipes here allow cakes to be stored at room temperature so that they can be safely displayed rather than having to keep them in the refrigerator until ready to be eaten. Ganache is usually used for chocolate-flavoured cakes.

Buttercream (frosting) and ganache are also used to seal and coat the cake before icing. They make a firm and perfectly smooth surface for the icing to sit on, filling in any gaps and imperfections in the cake.

BUTTERCREAM (FROSTING)

Makes about 500g (1lb 1½oz), enough for an 18–20cm (7–8in) round or square layered cake, or 20–24 cupcakes

MATERIALS
❖ 170g (6oz) unsalted or slightly salted butter, softened
❖ 340g (12oz) icing (confectioners') sugar
❖ 2 tablespoons water
❖ 1 teaspoon vanilla extract or alternative flavouring (see left)

EQUIPMENT
❖ Electric mixer
❖ Spatula

1 Put the butter and icing (confectioners') sugar in the bowl of an electric mixer and mix together, starting on a low speed to prevent the mixture from going everywhere.

2 Add the water and vanilla extract or other flavouring and increase the speed, beating the buttercream (frosting) really well until it becomes pale, light and fluffy.

3 Store the buttercream (frosting) for up to two weeks in the refrigerator in an airtight container.

Flavour variations

Lemon Add the finely grated zest of 1 lemon
Orange Add the finely grated zest of 1 orange
Chocolate Stir in 90g (3¼oz) melted white, milk or dark (semisweet or bittersweet) chocolate
Passion fruit Stir in 1 teaspoon strained and reduced passion fruit pulp
Coffee Add 1 teaspoon coffee extract
Almond Add a few drops of almond extract or to taste
Jams and conserves (jellies and preserves) can also be mixed in or used on top of a layer of buttercream (frosting), for example vanilla buttercream (frosting) and raspberry jam filling.

GANACHE

This rich, smooth filling is made from chocolate and cream. It is important to use good-quality chocolate, with at least 53 per cent cocoa solids, in order to achieve the best result.

Makes about 500g (1lb 1½oz), enough for an 18–20cm (7–8in) round or square layered cake, or 20–24 cupcakes

MATERIALS

❖ 250g (9oz) dark (semisweet or bittersweet) chocolate, chopped, or callets
❖ 250g (9oz) double (heavy) cream

EQUIPMENT

❖ Saucepan
❖ Mixing bowl
❖ Spatula

1 Put the chocolate in a bowl.

2 Bring the cream to the boil in a saucepan, then pour over the chocolate.

3 Stir until the chocolate has all melted and is perfectly combined with the cream. Leave to cool and cover.

4 Store for up to a week in the refrigerator.

TIP

Make sure that your ganache or buttercream (frosting) is at room temperature before you use it – you may even need to warm it slightly so that it spreads easily.

White chocolate ganache

White chocolate ganache is a nice alternative to buttercream (frosting) for heavy sponge cake fillings (cakes that have been made with extra flour). Use white chocolate in place of the dark (semisweet or bittersweet) chocolate and half the amount of cream. If you are making a small batch, melt the white chocolate before mixing with the hot cream.

SUGAR SYRUP

This is brushed on to the sponge to add moisture and flavour. The amount of syrup used is a personal choice. If you feel that your cake is quite dry, use more syrup. However, be aware that if you add too much syrup, your cake can become overly sweet and sticky. I recommend the following quantities for a 20cm (8in) layered round cake (you will need slightly more for a 20cm/8in square cake), 25 fondant fancies or 20–24 cupcakes.

MATERIALS

❖ 85g (3oz) caster (superfine) sugar

❖ 80ml (2³/₄fl oz) water

❖ Flavouring (optional – see below)

EQUIPMENT

❖ Saucepan

❖ Metal spoon

1 Put the sugar and water in a saucepan and bring to the boil, stirring once or twice.

2 Add any flavouring and leave to cool. Store in an airtight container in the refrigerator for up to one month.

TIP

Liqueurs such as Grand Marnier, amaretto and limoncello can also be added to enhance the syrup's flavour.

Flavourings

Vanilla Add 1 teaspoon good-quality vanilla extract
Lemon Replace the water with freshly squeezed, finely strained lemon juice
Orange Replace the water with freshly squeezed, finely strained orange juice

Cake portion guide

The following guide indicates about how many portions you get from the different sizes of cake. The number of portions are based on them being about 2.5cm (1in) square and 9cm (3½in) deep. You may choose to allow smaller portions for fruit cake, as it's a lot richer.

Size	10cm (4in)		13cm (5in)		15cm (6in)		18cm (7in)		20cm (8in)		23cm (9in)		25cm (10in)		28cm (11in)	
Shape	o	sq	o	sq	o	sq	o	sq	o	sq	o	sq	o	sq	o	sq
Portions	5	10	10	15	20	25	30	40	40	50	50	65	65	85	85	100

Filling and covering quantities

The chart below will give you a guide to how much buttercream (frosting) or ganache you need to layer and cover different-sized cakes and cupcakes (see Buttercream (Frosting) and Ganache).

Size	10cm (4in)	13cm (5in) 10–12 cupcakes	15cm (6in)	18cm (7in)	20cm (8in)	23cm (9in)	25cm (10in)	28cm (11in)
Buttercream (frosting) or ganache	175g (6oz)	250g (9oz)	350g (12½oz)	500g (1lb 1½oz)	650g (1lb 7oz)	800g (1lb 12oz)	1.1kg (2lb 7oz)	1.25kg (2lb 8oz)

BAKING & COVERING TECHNIQUES

PREPARING CAKE TINS

Before baking, you need to line the bottom and sides of the cake tin to prevent your cake from sticking.

1 Grease the inside of the tin with a little melted butter or sunflower oil spray first to help the paper stick and sit securely in the tin without curling up.

2 For round cakes, to line the bottom, lay your tin on a piece of greaseproof (wax) paper or baking parchment and draw around it using an edible pen. Cut on the inside of the line so that the circle is a good fit inside the tin. Put to one side. Cut a long strip of greaseproof (wax) paper or baking parchment at least 9cm (3½in) wide, fold over one of the long sides about 1cm (³⁄₈in) and crease firmly, then open out. Cut slits from the edge nearest to the fold up to the fold 2.5cm (1in) apart. Put the strip around the inside of tin, with the fold tucked into the bottom corner, then add the base circle and smooth down.

3 For square cakes, lay a piece of greaseproof (wax) paper or baking parchment over the top of the tin. Cut a square that overlaps it on each side by 7.5cm (3in). Cut a slit at each end on two opposite sides. Push the paper inside the tin and fold in the flaps.

LAYERING, FILLING AND PREPARATION

Preparing a cake for icing is one of the key processes in achieving a smooth and perfectly shaped cake. Sponge cakes usually consist of two or three layers (see Classic Sponge Cake), but fruit cakes are kept whole (see Traditional Fruit Cake).

MATERIALS
- ❖ Buttercream (frosting) or ganache (see Buttercream (Frosting) and Ganache), for filling and covering
- ❖ Sugar syrup (see Sugar Syrup), for brushing
- ❖ Jam or conserve (jelly or preserves), for filling (optional)

EQUIPMENT
- ❖ Cake leveller
- ❖ Large serrated knife
- ❖ Ruler
- ❖ Small, sharp paring knife (optional)
- ❖ Cake board, plus chopping board or large cake board if needed
- ❖ Turntable
- ❖ Palette knives
- ❖ Pastry brush

1 Cut the dark-baked crust from the base of your cakes. If you have two sponges of equal depths, use a cake leveller to cut them to the same height. If you have baked one-third of your cake mixture in one tin and two-thirds in the other, cut two layers from the deeper sponge with a large serrated knife or cake leveller so that you end up with three layers. Alternatively, you can cut three layers from a larger square cake, piecing together the third layer, as shown opposite. Your finished, prepared cake will be on a 1.25cm (½in) cake board, so the height of your sponge layers together should be about 9cm (3½in) deep.

2 You should have either baked your cake 2.5cm (1in) larger all round than required or baked a larger sponge (see Classic Sponge Cake). Cut around your cake board (this will be the size of your cake), cutting straight down without angling the knife inwards or outwards. For round cakes, use a small, sharp paring knife to do this and for square cakes use a large serrated one.

3 Once you have cut three layers of sponge, put them together to check that they are all even and level, trimming away any sponge if necessary. Place your base cake board on a turntable. If the board is smaller than the turntable, put a chopping board or another large cake board underneath. Use a non-slip mat if necessary.

4 Using a medium-sized palette knife, spread a small amount of buttercream (frosting) or ganache on to the cake board and stick down your bottom layer of sponge. Brush sugar syrup over the cake – how much will depend on how moist you would like your cake to be.

5 Evenly spread a layer of buttercream (frosting) or ganache about 3mm (1/8in) thick over the sponge, then a thin layer of jam or conserve (jelly or preserves) if you are using any.

6 Repeat this procedure for the next layer. Finish by adding the top layer and brushing with more sugar syrup.

TIP

Be careful not to add too much filling between the sponge layers as the cake will sink slightly under the weight of the icing and ridges will appear.

7 Cover the sides of the cake in buttercream (frosting) or ganache, then the top – you only need a very thin and even layer. If the coating becomes 'grainy' as it picks up crumbs from the cake, put it in the refrigerator to set for about 15 minutes and go over it again with a thin second coat. This undercoat is referred to as a 'crumb coat' and is often necessary for carved and sculpted cakes (see below), helping to seal the sponge.

8 Refrigerate your prepared cake for at least 1 hour so that it is firm before attempting to cover it with icing or marzipan; larger cakes will need a little longer.

CARVING AND SCULPTING CAKES

It is much easier to carve and sculpt cakes when they are very firm or almost frozen, so chill, wrapped in clingfilm (plastic wrap), in the freezer beforehand. This technique is used for the Groom's cake, and specific instructions are given with this project (see Here Comes the Groom!). When you come to carve or sculpt your cake, cut the sponge away little by little to prevent removing too much, especially if you are a beginner. Once you have achieved the desired shape, cover the cake with buttercream (frosting), or ganache if it's a chocolate cake, filling in any holes as you go (see above). Refrigerate until set and firm enough to cover with icing.

COVERING WITH MARZIPAN AND SUGARPASTE

Make sure that your cake is smoothly covered with buttercream (frosting) or ganache before you ice it (see above), because if there are any irregularities or imperfections left, you will see them through the icing. You can cover cakes with a second coat of icing if necessary, or cover your cake with a layer of marzipan before you ice it with sugarpaste (rolled fondant).

MATERIALS

❖ Marzipan (optional)

❖ Sugarpaste (rolled fondant)

❖ Icing (confectioners') sugar, for dusting (optional)

EQUIPMENT

❖ Greaseproof (wax) paper or baking parchment

❖ Scissors

❖ Large non-stick rolling pin

❖ Large non-stick board with non-slip mat (optional)

❖ Icing and marzipan spacers

❖ Needle scriber

❖ Icing smoother

❖ Small sharp knife

Round cakes

1 Cut a piece of greaseproof (wax) paper or baking parchment about 7.5cm (3in) larger all round than your cake and put the cake on top.

2 Knead your marzipan or sugarpaste (rolled fondant) until it is soft. Roll it out with a large non-stick rolling pin on a large non-stick board, which usually won't need dusting with icing (confectioners' sugar), set over a non-stick mat. Otherwise, just use a work surface dusted with icing (confectioners') sugar. Use the spacers to give you the correct width – about 5mm (3/16in). Lift the sugarpaste (rolled fondant) up with the rolling pin to release from the board and turn it a quarter turn before laying it back down to roll again. Try to keep it a round shape so that it will fit over your cake easily.

3 Pick the sugarpaste (rolled fondant) up on your rolling pin and lay it over your cake. Quickly but carefully use your hands to smooth it around and down the side of the cake. Pull the sugarpaste (rolled fondant) away from the side of the cake as you go until you reach the base. Try to push out any air bubbles that may occur or use a needle scriber to burst them carefully.

4 When the icing is on, use a smoother in a circular motion to go over the top of the cake. For the side of the cake, go around in forward circular movements, almost cutting the excess paste at the base. Trim the excess with a small sharp knife and use the smoother to go round the cake one final time to make sure that it is perfectly smooth.

Square cakes

Square cakes are iced in a similar way to round cakes, but pay attention to the corners to ensure that the icing doesn't tear. Use your hands to carefully cup the icing around the corners before you start working it down the sides. Mend any tears with clean soft icing as soon as possible so that the icing blends together well.

TIP

You need to work quite quickly with icing, as it will soon start to dry out and crack. Keep any leftover icing well wrapped in a plastic bag to prevent it from drying out.

ICING CAKE BOARDS

Covering the base cake board with icing makes a huge difference to the finished cake, giving it a clean, professional finish. By carefully choosing the right colour for the icing, the board can be incorporated into the design of the cake itself.

Moisten the board with some water. Roll out the sugarpaste (rolled fondant) to 4mm (a generous ⅛in), ideally using icing or marzipan spacers. Pick the icing up on the rolling pin and lay it over the cake board. Place the board either on a turntable or bring it towards the edge of the work surface so that the icing is hanging down over it. Use your icing smoother in a downwards motion to cut a smooth edge around the board. Cut away any excess. Finish by smoothing the top using circular movements to achieve a flat and perfectly smooth surface for your cake to sit on. Leave to dry overnight.

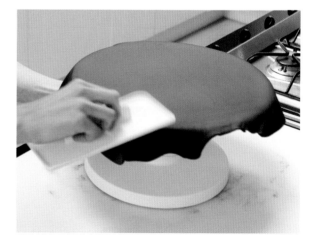

Marzipan and sugarpaste quantities

This following charts give an estimate of the quantities you will need to cover different-sized cakes and cake boards; square cakes will require slightly more than round cakes. If you are not very experienced at covering cakes, allow a bit extra than specified here. These quantities are based on cakes about 9cm (3½in) deep. For deeper cakes, simply use a bit more icing.

COVERING CAKES

Cake size	15cm (6in)	18cm (7in)	20cm (8in)	23cm (9in)	25cm (10in)	28cm (11in)	30cm (12in)	35cm (14in)
Covering cake (marzipan/ sugarpaste)	650g (1lb 7oz)	750g (1lb 10oz)	850g (1lb 14oz)	1kg (2lb 3½oz)	1.25kg (2lb 12oz)	1.5kg (3lb 5oz)	1.75kg (3lb 13oz)	2.25kg (5lb)

COVERING CAKE BOARDS

Cake board size	23cm (9in)	25cm (10in)	28cm (11in)	30cm (12in)	33cm (13in)	35cm (14in)	40cm (16in)
Icing cake board	600g (1lb 5oz)	650g (1lb 7oz)	725g (1lb 9½oz)	850g (1lb 14oz)	1kg (2lb 3½oz)	1.2kg (2lb 11oz)	1.5kg (3lb 5oz)

SECURING RIBBON AROUND CAKE BOARDS

To finish your cake off in style, attach some double-faced satin ribbon around the board to coordinate with the cake design and colour scheme. I use 15mm (5⁄8in) -wide ribbon for this. Stick the ribbon in place with double-sided tape at intervals around the board.

TIP

For square cakes, put the double-sided tape around each corner, as well as a small piece in the centre of each side.

ASSEMBLING TIERED CAKES

Stacking cakes on top of one another is not a difficult process, but it needs to be done in the right way so that you can rest assured that the cake is structurally sound. I prefer to use hollow plastic dowels, as they are very sturdy and easily cut to the correct height. Thinner plastic dowels can be used for smaller cakes. As a general guide, use three dowels for a round cake and four for square. Use more dowels for larger cakes.

MATERIALS

❖ Stiff royal icing (see Royal Icing)

❖ Iced cake board (see Icing Cake Boards)

EQUIPMENT

❖ Cake-top marking template

❖ Needle scriber or marking tool

❖ Hollow plastic dowels

❖ Edible pen

❖ Large serrated knife

❖ Spare cake board

❖ Spirit level

❖ Icing smoothers

1 Use the cake-top marking template to find the centre of your base cake.

2 Using a needle scriber or marking tool, mark the cake where the dowels should go. These need to be positioned well inside the diameter of the cake to be stacked on top.

3 Push a dowel into the cake where it has been marked. Using an edible pen, mark the dowel where it meets the top of the cake.

TIP

If your cake is slightly uneven, push the dowel into the tallest part of the cake.

4 Remove the dowel and cut it at the mark with a serrated knife. Cut the other dowels to the same height and insert them all into the cake. Place a cake board on top of the dowels and check that they are equal in height by using a spirit level on the board.

5 Stick your base cake on to the centre of your iced cake board with some stiff royal icing. Use your smoothers to move it into position if necessary. Allow the icing to set for a few minutes before stacking on the next tier. Repeat to attach a third tier, if using.

TIP

'Dummy' or fake tiers are often used for wedding cakes to make cakes bigger without having too much cake! These do not need dowelling.

DOWELS
The number of dowels in each tier really depends on the amount and sizes of the cakes that are going to be stacked on top of them. Please see the chart below for a guide.

Cake size	15cm (6in)	20cm (8in)	25cm (10in)	30cm (12in)	35cm (14in)
No. of dowels	3-4	3-4	4-5	5-6	8

MINIATURE CAKES

These cakes are cut from larger pieces of cake (see Cake Recipes) and are layered, filled and iced in a similar fashion to the larger cakes. Bake a square cake and cut your cakes from this, either round or square. The size of the cake will depend on how many cakes you require and the size you would like them to be. Always choose a slightly larger size of cake than you need to allow for wastage. For nine 5cm (2in) square mini cakes (I usually make them this size), you would need an 18cm (7in) square cake. Use only two-thirds of the quantities of ingredients in the charts, as mini cakes are not as deep as large cakes. Bake all the mixture in one tin rather than dividing it between two for larger cakes.

MATERIALS

✤ Large square baked classic sponge cake or classic chocolate cake (see Cake Recipes)
✤ Sugar syrup (see Sugar Syrup)
✤ Buttercream (frosting) or ganache (see Buttercream (Frosting) and Ganache)
✤ Sugarpaste (rolled fondant)

EQUIPMENT

✤ Cake leveller
✤ Circle cutter or serrated knife
✤ Pastry brush
✤ Cake card (optional)
✤ Palette knife
✤ Large non-stick rolling pin
✤ Large non-stick board with non-slip mat
✤ Metal ruler
✤ Large sharp knife
✤ Large circle cutter or small sharp knife
✤ 2 icing smoothers

TIP

For mini traditional fruit cakes, bake the mixture in small, individual tins, as they can't be cut out due to the structure of the cakes.

TIP

It's much easier to work with the sponge if it's very cold, as it will be a good deal firmer.

Miniature Square Cakes

Square mini cakes are iced in a similar way to round ones. Use a sharp knife to cut away the excess icing. Use smoothers on opposite sides to press and smooth the icing around the four sides.

1 Slice your large square cake horizontally into two even layers using a cake leveller. Cut small individual rounds (using a cutter) or squares (using a serrated knife).

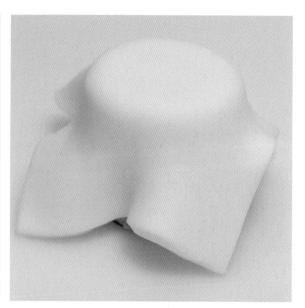

2 Brush the pieces of sponge with sugar syrup and sandwich together with either buttercream (frosting), or ganache if using a chocolate-flavoured cake. It is easier if you stick the bottom piece of cake to a cake card the same size and shape as your mini cake, using buttercream (frosting) or ganache, but not essential. Working quickly, pick up each cake and cover the sides evenly with buttercream (frosting) or ganache. Finish by covering the top and then place the cakes in the refrigerator for at least 20 minutes to firm up.

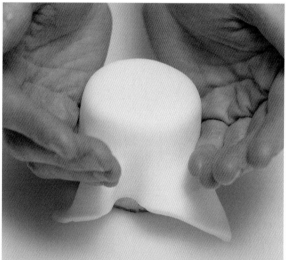

3 Roll out a piece of sugarpaste (rolled fondant) 38cm (15in) square and 5mm (³/₁₆in) thick with a large non-stick rolling pin on a large non-stick board set over a non-slip mat. Cut nine small squares and lay one over each cake. If you are a beginner, prepare half the cakes at a time, keeping the other squares under clingfilm (plastic wrap) to prevent them drying out.

4 Use your hands to work the icing down around the sides of the cake and trim away the excess with a large circle cutter or small sharp knife.

5 Use two icing smoothers on either side of the cake going forwards and backwards and turning the cake as you go to create a perfectly smooth result. Leave the icing to dry, ideally overnight, before decorating the cakes.

BAKING CUPCAKES

Cupcakes are made in exactly the same way as the classic sponge cake, classic chocolate cake or carrot cake (see Cake Recipes). The amount of ingredients you need will depend on the size of your cases. For 10–12 cupcakes, use the quantities given for a 13cm (5in) round or 10cm (4in) square cake. Use cupcakes cases (liners) to bake the mixture, placing them in tartlet tins or muffin trays and filling two-thirds to three-quarters full. Bake in a preheated oven at 180°C/350°F/Gas Mark 4 for about 20 minutes until springy to the touch.

Cupcake cases (liners) come in plain or patterned paper, or in foil in a range of colours. I prefer to use plain foil ones, as they keep the cakes fresh and don't detract from the decoration on the cakes. But you can use decorative cases (liners) for plainer cupcakes.

Cupcakes can be iced in various ways, depending on the look and taste you want to achieve. While some techniques are more involved and a little tricky to accomplish, others are much simpler and are a great way to get the children involved.

COVERING CUPCAKES WITH SUGARPASTE

Sugarpaste (rolled fondant icing) -covered cakes are quick to do. You can just cut a circle to fit inside the cupcake top but I prefer to cover the cake completely and go right up to the edge. Use cupcakes that have a nice domed shape to them.

1 Using a palette knife, spread a thin layer of flavoured buttercream (frosting) or ganache over the cakes so that it forms a perfectly rounded and smooth surface for the icing to sit on. Refrigerate the cupcakes for 20 minutes or so until they are firm.

2 Roll out some sugarpaste (rolled fondant) and, using a circle cutter, cut out circles slightly bigger than the cupcake top. I would suggest cutting out nine at a time. Cover any circles you are not using with clingfilm (plastic wrap). One at a time, drape the icing circles over the cupcake and use the smoother to cut away the overhanging paste around the sides. Smooth all the way over and around.

FONDANT-DIPPED CUPCAKES

This way of decorating cupcakes is much more involved, but liquid fondant really makes a delicious and lovely looking little cake. I have used ready-made fondant here, which you can buy from specialist suppliers, but you can use a powdered fondant instead, available from most good supermarkets.

1 Shave off any uneven bumps with a small, sharp serrated knife so that the cakes are perfectly shaped. Brush the tops with the flavoured sugar syrup.

2 Bring the apricot masking spread or strained jam (jelly) to the boil in a saucepan and leave to cool slightly before brushing over the cupcakes with a pastry brush. Refrigerate for at least 15–30 minutes.

3 Put the fondant in a microwave-proof bowl and warm in the microwave for about 1½ minutes on medium power until it can be easily poured.

4 Add the glucose and three-quarters of the unflavoured sugar syrup and gently stir together, trying to avoid introducing too many air bubbles. Add any colouring. If you are dipping cakes in more than one colour, split the fondant between two or more bowls beforehand. Cover the bowl or bowls you are not using immediately with clingfilm (plastic wrap).

MATERIALS (MAKES 20)

❖ 20 domed-shaped cupcakes (see opposite)

❖ 1 quantity sugar syrup, flavoured to match the sponge, and 1 quantity unflavoured (see Sugar Syrup)

❖ 100g (3½oz) apricot masking spread or strained jam (jelly)

❖ 1kg (2lb 4oz) tub ready-made fondant

❖ 1 tablespoon liquid glucose

❖ Food colouring, as required

EQUIPMENT

❖ Small, sharp serrated knife

❖ Pastry brush

❖ Microwave oven and microwave-proof bowl

❖ 2 metal spoons or palette knife

5 Return the fondant to the microwave and heat it gently until slightly warmer than body temperature (39–40°C/102–104°F). Test the consistency by dipping one of the cupcakes into the fondant. If it is too thick, add the remaining unflavoured sugar syrup until the fondant coats the cupcake well. Be careful not make it too runny or the fondant won't set.

6 Dip the tops of the cupcakes one at a time in the fondant, holding the cake by its case (liner). Allow the excess to drip down for a second and turn it back up the right way to set. Once you have dipped all the cupcakes, you may need to give them a second coating; wait 5–10 minutes for the first coat to dry.

FONDANT FANCIES

These are a great alternative to cupcakes. Like the mini cakes (see Miniature Cakes), they are cut from a square or rectangular classic sponge cake (see Classic Sponge Cake) and can be a variety of shapes, although the easiest to make are square. If they are to fit in a cupcake case (liner), they should be about 4cm (1½in) square and 4cm (1½in) high. Bake shallow cakes (see Materials right) and trim the top and bottom to give you the correct height. Vanilla, lemon or orange-flavoured sponge works best for fondant fancies.

The fondant icing is prepared in the same way as for the cupcakes (see Baking Cupcakes), but the technique used when dipping them is quite different.

1 Once you have layered, filled and stuck the sponge back together, brush the remaining flavoured sugar syrup over the top of the sponge before covering it with a thin layer of the apricot masking spread or jam (jelly).

MATERIALS (MAKES 16)

❖ 18cm (7in) square shallow classic sponge cake (see Classic Sponge Cake, but use half the quantities specified), split into two layers and filled with jam (jelly), marmalade or lemon, lime or orange curd (see Layering, Filling and Preparation)

❖ 1 quantity sugar syrup, flavoured to match the sponge, and 1 quantity unflavoured (see Sugar Syrup)

❖ 2 tablespoons apricot masking spread or strained jam (jelly), boiled and slightly cooled

❖ 175g (6oz) marzipan or sugarpaste (rolled fondant)

❖ 750g (1lb 10½oz) ready-made fondant

❖ ¾ tablespoon liquid glucose

❖ Food colouring, as required

EQUIPMENT

❖ Pastry brush
❖ Large non-stick rolling pin
❖ Large non-stick board with non-slip mat
❖ Icing or marzipan spacers
❖ Icing smoothers
❖ Metal ruler
❖ Large and small sharp knife
❖ Dipping fork
❖ Wire rack
❖ 16 cupcake cases (liners)

2 Roll the marzipan or sugarpaste (rolled fondant) out with a large non-stick rolling pin on a large non-stick board set over a non-slip mat to 3–4mm (1/8in) thick, using the spacers to guide you. Lay it over your sponge and run the smoother over the top so that it is firmly stuck down. Mark and cut 4cm (1½in) squares with a sharp knife, keeping the squares together until you are ready to dip them. Place the sponge in the refrigerator and chill for at least 1 hour.

3 Prepare the fondant by following Steps 3–5 for Fondant-Dipped Cupcakes, using the unflavoured sugar syrup.

4 Cut away any excess trimmings from the sponge. Plunge each square fancy, marzipan/icing side down, into your warm fondant. Working quickly, use the dipping fork to turn the fancy back upwards and move it across to the wire rack to allow the excess icing to drip down and off the sides of the cake. Repeat for each fancy.

5 Remove the fancies from the rack using a small sharp knife to cut away any excess fondant.

6 Place each fancy into a cupcake case (liner) that has been slightly pressed out beforehand so that the cake fits easily inside. Cup the case (liner) back up around the sides of the cake so that it takes on its shape. Place the fancies together, side by side, until they are completely set and ready to decorate.

BAKING COOKIES

Cookies are great fun to make – ideal for getting children involved – and are suitable for just about any occasion. You can cut out any shapes from the cookie dough and decorate them however you like. In this book, you will learn how to use a variety of techniques to create eye-catching and delicious treats that are sure to impress.

MATERIALS (MAKES 10–15 LARGE OR 25–30 MEDIUM)

- ❖ 250g (9oz) unsalted butter
- ❖ 250g (9oz) caster (superfine) sugar
- ❖ 1–2 medium eggs
- ❖ 1 teaspoon vanilla extract
- ❖ 500g (1lb 1½oz) plain (all-purpose) flour, plus extra for dusting

EQUIPMENT

- ❖ Large electric mixer
- ❖ Spatula
- ❖ Deep tray or plastic container
- ❖ Clingfilm (plastic wrap)
- ❖ Rolling pin
- ❖ Cookie cutters or templates
- ❖ Sharp knife (if using templates)
- ❖ Baking trays
- ❖ Greaseproof (wax) paper or baking parchment

TIP

The cookie dough can be made up to two weeks ahead or stored in the freezer until ready to use.

1 In a bowl of an electric mixer, beat the butter and sugar together until creamy and quite fluffy.

2 Add the eggs and vanilla extract and mix until they are well combined.

3 Sift the flour, add to the bowl and mix until all the ingredients just come together. You may need to do this in two stages – do not over-mix.

4 Tip the dough into a container lined with clingfilm (plastic wrap) and press down firmly. Cover with clingfilm (plastic wrap) and refrigerate for at least 30 minutes.

5 On a work surface lightly dusted with flour, roll out the cookie dough to about 4mm (1/8in) thick. Sprinkle a little extra flour on top of the dough as you roll to prevent it from sticking to the rolling pin.

TIP

Be careful not too add too much flour when you are rolling out your dough, as it will become too dry.

6 Cut out your shapes either with cutters or using templates and a sharp knife. Place on baking trays lined with greaseproof (wax) paper or baking parchment and return to the refrigerator to rest for at least 30 minutes.

7 Bake the cookies in a preheated oven at 180°C/350°F/Gas Mark 4 for about 10 minutes, depending on their size, or until they are golden brown. Leave them to cool completely before storing them in an airtight container until you are ready to decorate them. The baked cookies will keep for up to one month.

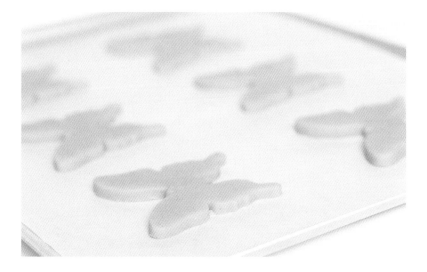

Flavour variations

Chocolate Substitute 50g (1¾oz) flour with cocoa powder (unsweetened cocoa).
Citrus Add the finely grated zest of 1 lemon or orange.
Almond Replace the vanilla extract with 1 teaspoon almond extract.

DECORATING TECHNIQUES

ROYAL ICING

Working with royal icing is one of the most useful skills to learn in cake decorating. It is a highly versatile medium, as it can be used for icing cakes and cookies, for intricate piping of decorations (borders, flowers and lettering) or for simply attaching and sticking.

The icing is best used as fresh as possible, but it will keep for up to five days in an airtight container. Re-beat the mixture back to its correct consistency before use if it is not used immediately.

MATERIALS
❖ 2 medium egg whites or 15g (½oz) dried egg albumen powder mixed with 75ml (2½fl oz) water
❖ 500g (1lb 1½oz) icing (confectioners') sugar

EQUIPMENT
❖ Large electric mixer
❖ Sieve (strainer)
❖ Spatula

1 If using dried egg powder, soak the powder in the water for at least 30 minutes in advance, but ideally overnight in the refrigerator.

2 Sift the icing (confectioners') sugar into the mixing bowl of an electric mixer and add the egg whites or strained reconstituted egg mixture.

3 Mix together on a low speed for about 3–4 minutes until the icing has reached a stiff-peak consistency, which is what you need for sticking on decorations and gluing cakes together.

4 Store the icing in an airtight container covered with a damp, clean cloth to prevent it from drying out.

Soft-peak royal icing

In order to pipe various patterns and decorations easily, you may need to add a tiny amount of water to your royal icing so that the consistency is a bit softer.

'RUN-OUT' ICING

Royal icing is thinned down with more water to 'flood' (fill in) cookies (see opposite). For the desired consistency, test the icing by lifting your spoon and letting the icing drip back into the bowl. The icing falling back into the bowl should remain on the surface for five seconds before disappearing. If it is too runny it will run over the outlines and sides of the cookies, but if it is too stiff it won't spread very well.

ROYAL-ICED COOKIES

This is my favourite method of icing cookies, as I love the taste of the crisp white icing against the softer texture of the cookie underneath. Most of the cookie projects in this book have been iced this way. If you are icing a large quantity of cookies, use a squeezable plastic bottle with a small tube instead of piping (pastry) bags.

MATERIALS

❧ Soft-peak royal icing (see opposite)

EQUIPMENT

❧ Paper piping (pastry) bags, small and large (see Making a Piping (Pastry) Bag)

❧ Piping tubes (tips): nos. 1 and 1.5 or 2

TIP

If the area you need to 'flood' is relatively large, work round the edges of the piped outline and then work inwards to the centre to ensure an even covering.

1 Place the no. 1.5 or 2 tube (tip) in a small piping (pastry) bag and fill with some soft-peak royal icing. Pipe an outline around the edge of each cookie.

2 Thin down some more royal icing with water until 'flooding' consistency (see Royal Icing) and place in a large piping (pastry) bag fitted with the no. 1 tube. Use to flood inside the outlines on the cookies with icing. For larger cookies or 'run-outs' (see 'Run-Out' Icing), you can snip off the tip of the bag instead of using a tube (tip).

3 Once dry, pipe over any details that are required and stick on any decorations.

COVERING COOKIES WITH SUGARPASTE

This is a very simple and quick way to ice cookies, yet still looks really neat and effective. Roll out some sugarpaste (rolled fondant) to no more than 4mm (1/8in) thick and cut out the shape of the cookie using the same cutter or template used for the cookie dough. Stick the icing on to the cookie using boiled and cooled apricot masking spread or strained jam (jelly), taking care not to stretch it out of shape.

MAKING A PIPING (PASTRY) BAG

1 Cut two equal triangles from a large square of greaseproof (wax) paper or baking parchment. As a guide, for small bags cut from a 15–20cm (6–8in) square and for large bags cut from a 30–35cm (12–14in) square.

2 Keeping the centre point towards you with the longest side furthest away, curl the right-hand corner inwards and bring the point to meet the centre point. Adjust your hold so that you have the two points together between your right thumb and index finger.

3 With your left hand, curl the left point inwards, bringing it across the front and around to the back of the other two points in the centre of the cone. Adjust your grip again so that you are now holding the three points together with both thumbs and index fingers.

4 Tighten the cone-shaped bag by gently rubbing your thumb and index fingers forwards and backwards until you have a sharp tip at the end of the bag.

5 Carefully fold the back of the bag (where all the points meet) inwards, making sure that you press hard along the fold. Repeat this to ensure that it is really secure.

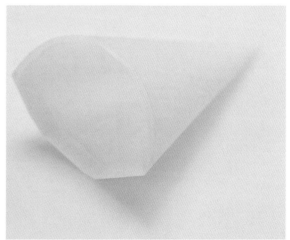

TIP

Make lots of piping (pastry) bags at a time and put them aside for a decorating session.

PIPING WITH ROYAL ICING

For basic piping work, use soft-peak royal icing (see Royal Icing). The size of the tube (tip) you use will depend on the job at hand and how competent you are.

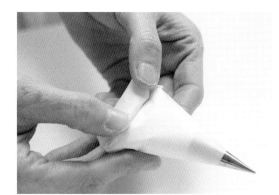

Fill the piping (pastry) bag until it is no more than one-third full. Fold the top over, away from the join, until you have a tight and well-sealed bag. The correct way to hold the piping (pastry) bag is important. Use your index finger to guide the bag. You can also use your other hand to guide you if it's easier.

To pipe dots, squeeze the icing out gently until you have the dot that's the size you want. Stop squeezing, then lift the bag. If there is a peak in the icing, use a damp brush to flatten it down.

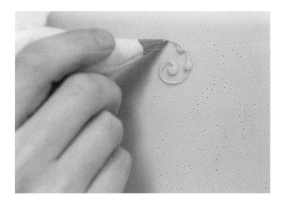

To pipe teardrops, once you have squeezed out the dot, pull the tube (tip) through the dot, then release the pressure and lift the bag. To pipe elongated teardrops and swirls, squeeze out a ball of icing and drag the icing round to one side to form a swirl or scroll. Increase the pressure and amount of icing you squeeze out for longer, larger shapes. Keeping close to the surface you are piping on is known as 'scratch piping'.

To pipes lines, touch the tube (tip) down, then lift the bag up in a smooth movement, squeezing gently. Decrease the pressure and touch it back down to the point where you want the line to finish. Try not to drag the icing along, or it will become uneven. Use a template or a cookie outline as a guide where possible.

To pipe a 'snail trail' border, squeeze out a large dot of icing and drag the tube (tip) through it to one side like a teardrop. Repeat this motion around the cake.

WORKING WITH FLOWER PASTE

Flower (petal/gum) paste is used for creating more delicate decorations for cakes and cookies, such as flowers, frills, bows and streamers, as it can be rolled out really thinly. Before using, knead the paste well by continuously pulling it apart with your fingers.

MODELLING PASTE AND CMC

Modelling paste is basically a stiffer version of sugarpaste (rolled fondant), which enables you to mould larger, less delicate shapes and objects. It isn't as strong and won't dry out as quickly as flower (petal/gum) paste. You can buy ready-made modelling paste, but it is really simple and cheaper to make your own using CMC (sodium carboxymethyl cellulose). This comes in the form of a powder, which you knead into the sugarpaste (rolled fondant); use about 1 teaspoon per 300g (10½oz) icing.

TIP

Always add your colouring gradually and keep some extra white icing to hand in case you make a mistake.

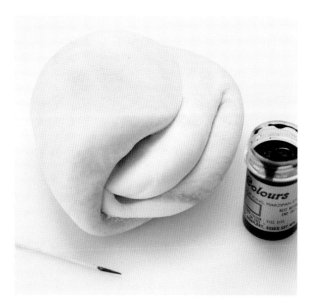

COLOURING ICINGS

There are two types of colouring used to colour icing: paste and liquid. I prefer to use food paste colours, especially when colouring sugarpaste (rolled fondant), flower (petal/gum) paste and marzipan, to prevent the icing from becoming too wet and sticky. Small amounts can be added with a cocktail stick (toothpick) and larger amounts with a knife, then kneaded into the icing. Liquid colours work well with royal icing and liquid fondant, but be careful not to add too much too soon.

Be aware that the colour of your icing can often change as it dries. Some colours tend to fade, while others darken.

TIP

It's always advisable to colour more icing than you need to allow for any mishaps, and quantities given in the recipes are generous. Any leftovers can be stored in an airtight bag in a sealed container for future use.

TEMPLATES

(All shown at 50% of actual size. Enlarge by 200% to use.)

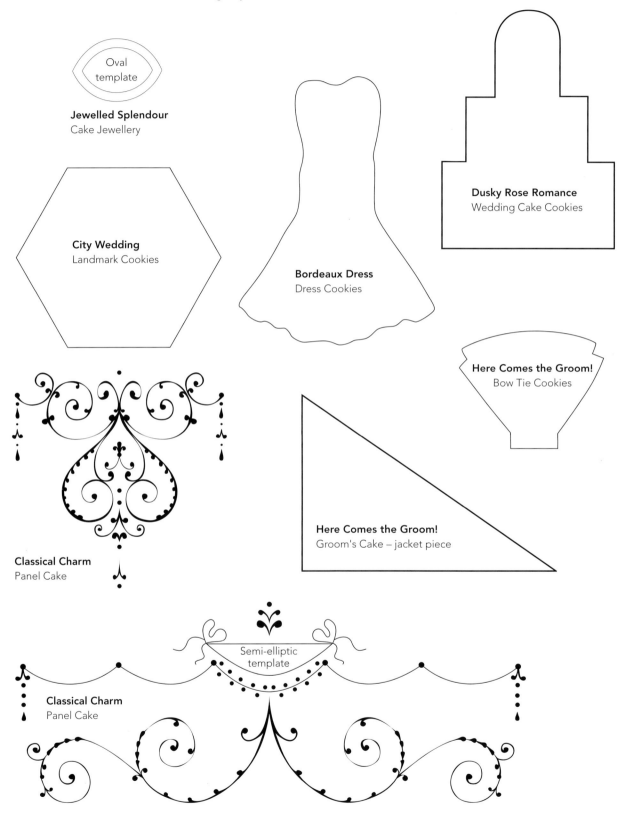

Oval
template

Jewelled Splendour
Cake Jewellery

City Wedding
Landmark Cookies

Bordeaux Dress
Dress Cookies

Dusky Rose Romance
Wedding Cake Cookies

Here Comes the Groom!
Bow Tie Cookies

Classical Charm
Panel Cake

Here Comes the Groom!
Groom's Cake – jacket piece

Semi-elliptic
template

Classical Charm
Panel Cake

SUPPLIERS

UK

The Cake Parlour
www.thecakeparlour.com
146 Arthur Road, London,
SW19 8AQ
Tel: 020 8947 4424

FMM Sugarcraft
www.fmmsugarcraft.com
Unit 7, Chancerygate Business
Park, Whiteleaf Road, Hemel
Hempstead, Herts, HP3 9HD
Tel: 01442 292970

Orchard Products
www.orchardproducts.co.uk
51 Hallyburton Road, Hove,
East Sussex, BN3 7GP
Tel: 01273 419418

Squire's Kitchen Shop
www.squires-shop.com
3 Waverley Lane, Farnham,
Surrey, GU9 8BB
Tel: 0845 225 5671

Sugarshack
www.sugarshack.co.uk
Unit 12, Bowmans Trading Estate,
Westmoreland Road,
London, NW9 9RL
Tel: 020 8204 2994

US

Designer Stencils
www.designerstencils.com
Designer Stencils, 2503 Silverside
Road, Wilmington, DE 19810
Tel: 800-822-7836

Global Sugar Art
www.globalsugarart.com
625 Route 3, Unit 3, Plattsburgh,
New York 12901
Tel: 1-518-561-3039

CREDITS

The author and the publisher would like to thank the following:

The British Academy
10-11 Carlton House Terrace,
London, SW1Y 5AH
www.10-11cht.com

Burlington Berties
329 Haydons Road,
Wimbledon,
London, SW19 8LA
www.burlingtonberties.
co.uk

Caroline Castigliano
154 Brompton Road,
Knightsbridge,
London, SW3 1HX
www.carolinecastigliano.
co.uk

Claire Pettibone
Blackburn Bridal Couture Ltd,
56 Tranquil Vale,
Blackheath,
London, SE3 0BD
www.blackburnbridal.co.uk

The Crockery Cupboard
www.thecrockerycupboard.
co.uk

Cutture London
269 Wandsworth Bridge
Road,
London, SW6 2TX
www.cutture.com

Dottie Creations
Forest Lodge,
161 Creek Road,
March,
Cambridgeshire, PE15 8RY
www.dottiecreations.com

Emmy Shoes
65 Cross Street,
Islington,
London, N1 2BB
www.emmyshoes.co.uk

Farrow & Ball
www.farrow-ball.com

Jones Hire
24 Creekside,
Deptford,
London, SE8 3DZ
www.joneshire.co.uk

Lisbeth Dahl
www.lisbethdahl.dk

Marc Wallace Kings Road
261 New Kings Road,
London, SW6 4RB
www.marcwallace.com

Nicki MacFarlane
www.nickimacfarlane.com

Rayners Catering Hire
Banquet House,
118-120 Garratt Lane,
London, SW18 4DJ
www.rayners.co.uk

**Simply Elegant
(Elizabeth Gall)**
25 Sparrow Drive,
Orpington,
Kent, BR5 1RY
www.simplyelegant.co.uk

Zita Elze
287 Sandycombe Road,
Kew,
Richmond,
Surrey, TW9 3LU
www.zitaelze.com

ACKNOWLEDGMENTS

First of all, I would like to thank all the wonderful people who have supplied me with their marvellous products, which have been the inspirations behind the cake designs in this book: Claire Pettibone and Caroline Castigliano for the stunning bridal gowns; Dottie Creations and Cutture for their unique stationery, the lovely Emmy for her gorgeous shoes; Marc Wallace for the fabulous tuxedo; Nicki Macfarlane for the delightful flower girl dress; 10-Carlton Terrace for allowing us to shoot in your beautiful venue; Elizabeth Gall for supplying all the balloons; and Zita Elze for such amazing flowers, as always.

Huge thanks also to the following suppliers who sent such wonderful props and tableware: Lisbeth Dahl, Jones Hire, The Crockery Cupboard and Rayners Catering Supplies; and to Farrow & Ball for the stunning wallpapers on pages 29, 37, 45 and 61.

I'd also like to thank Sarah Underhill and the rest of the team at David and Charles for all their help, Sian Irvine for the photography and Heather Haynes for all her editing, patience and perseverance.

Finally, thanks so much to my friend and assistant Roubina 'Beanpod' for her cake advice and help, and to my amazing family who have supported me as always.

INDEX

ABOUT THE AUTHOR

After being inspired by making her own wedding cake in 2005, Zoe turned passion into profession and headed to London to work with some of the most prestigious bakers in the business. Along the way she developed her unique style and skills, and subsequently set up her own business in 2008. Zoe's cake creations have drawn attention from both clients and the press, and she was awarded *Perfect Wedding*'s 'Best Wedding Cake Designer 2010' award. Zoe has previously published three titles for D&C. Following her success, Zoe opened a boutique in Wimbledon, London called The Cake Parlour, which continues to make wedding cakes a year later. As a result of the popularity of Zoe's books, she also runs cake decorating classes for all levels of students.

www.thecakeparlour.com
www.zoeclarkcakes.com